John Bramham was born in 1944. He graduated from Manchester University in 1966 with a degree in Psychology and then studied Personnel Management at Leeds Polytechnic.

He joined North Eastern Gas in Leeds and after training worked in industrial relations and other areas of personnel work. In 1973 he moved to the headquarters of British Gas as Manpower Planning Manager before becoming Industrial Relations Manager in the Northern Region. He is now Director of Personnel, North Eastern Region.

John Bramham is married and has two daughters. His chief hobbies are gardening, making films, teaching chess, education and visiting the countryside.

His previous book on *Practical Manpower Planning*, first published in 1975, has long been established as a standard text. It was described by the *British Journal of Administrative Management* as 'extremely easy to read': 'the author is to be congratulated on presenting such a daunting topic in such a clear and thought-provoking manner'.

To

Bob and Charlotte, Joan and Kris, who may yet see the principles in which they believe applied as second nature at work.

The Institute of Personnel and Development is the leading publisher of books and reports for personnel and training professionals and students and for all those concerned with the effective management and development of people at work. For full details of all our titles please telephone the Publishing Department on 081 946 9100.

Human Resource Planning

John Bramham

Second edition

Institute of Personnel and Development

First Published 1989
Second edition 1994

Photoset by The Comp-Room, Aylesbury
and printed in Great Britain by
The Cromwell Press, Wiltshire.

British Library Cataloguing in Publication Data
Bramham, John
  Human Resource Planning. – 2Rev.ed
  I. Title
  658.301

ISBN 0-85292-554-9

**INSTITUTE OF PERSONNEL
AND DEVELOPMENT**

IPD House, Camp Road, London SW19 4UX
Tel: 081 946 9100   Fax: 081 947 2570
Registered office as above. Registered Charity No. 1038333
A company limited by guarantee. Registered in England No. 2931892

Contents

Acknowledgements

I should first recognize the debt I owe to all those 'excellence' writers who have encouraged my inclination to believe in people and to root such an approach in pride in a job well done. I have met some of these people, and their writings and words have excited me and sent my mind racing.

There are many friends and colleagues in British Gas, the Manpower Society and the Institute of Personnel Management (IPM) who have helped form these ideas and will continue to do so. The late Dan Gowler and Janine Nahapiet of Templeton College, Oxford require particular mention. To Allan McKay should go thanks for allowing me the space to develop many of these ideas as his Regional Director of Personnel in Leeds.

My thanks are also due to John Walmsley, Peter Joy, Dave Cox and Jeff Bakes who read the first text. Matthew Reisz, of the Publications Department of the IPM, guided with patience and professionalism the production of the second text. I should also mention Caron Carnachan who gave so much of her own time to prepare and amend the revised typescript.

Finally, what is written is my own responsibility and the opinions and ideas will not always coincide with those of British Gas or the IPM.

JOHN BRAMHAM

Preface

This text sets out some ideas which are part of the developing conceptual framework of human resourcing (HR). A discussion of the 'old wine in new bottles' argument recognizes that there will be those who, through inability to change or cynicism, will seek to use HR 'strategies' to mask the conflicts and tensions of an organization that has not or cannot change the way the people it employs are managed.

And this is the key. Uncertainty, even ambiguity, in a fluid and demanding world means that employees have to take centre stage as key players in the development of organizational success. The text recognizes that success for organizations will still be measured in financial and economic terms but that the way people are managed will for many organizations make all the difference.

For these reasons I stress development and learning to ensure that people give their best and enjoy giving it. Underlying this is the concept of the 'learning organization' which is being admirably supported through such initiatives as the TEC's (Training & Enterprise Councils) 'Investors in People' initiative. Organization design is discussed to ensure that leaner, fitter and flatter structures avoid the barriers to creativity, fulfilment and change of the traditional, multi-layered, territorially disputed structure. This leads to empowerment – although a 'health warning' is also attached to this strategy. These concepts are seen as supported by essential ingredients of HR such as equality, motivation, flexibility, objective setting, performance and productivity and are all backed up by a reward structure which lays greater emphasis on variety and differential payment to reward individual as well as collective excellence.

These aspects, in turn, are related to employee relations in an HR environment and to the need to build committed and communicating teams. At the same time, the organization must find new ways of finding what people want and think. Opinion surveys are seen as having a contribution, if backed up by an approach such as two-way team briefing to ensure that employees are kept informed. The question of a trade union role in HR is discussed, with a recognition that old-style collectivist and combative approaches are inappropriate in organizations where people are seen as the key to organizational and economic success. The differences from manpower planning are explored and the simple switch from 'manpower planning' to 'human resource planning' is rejected (as is the retitling of 'personnel management' to read 'human resource management') without change in either content or context. The role of leadership is explored, particularly the recognition of power concepts as a key feature of any, but particularly of HR, management.

Finally, underpinning everything is service and quality. In these aspects is also seen the hope for personal fulfilment – the pride in a job well done – that has apparently been lost for many people. At the same time, this would ensure that the fundamental consideration of the continuity of the organization does not conflict with the continuity of the employee.

The organization's personnel function must move to embrace these ideas. Human resourcing is an approach to the management of people at work. It goes beyond what has gone before in that, intertwined and together with customers and quality, it leads to the three pillars of the modern organization. There is still some concern about the opportunity the subject provides for new jargon (what is cynically dubbed 'HR-speak') but I put my faith in people and hope for an end to traditional personnel management with its emphasis on bureaucracy, controls, policing, procedures, rules and handbooks.

It may be an uncertain future, even chaotic, but it will allow people to be creative and will be, given a mind for it, fun!

JOHN BRAMHAM
Leeds

Chapter 1

Human Resourcing – Personnel Management for the Future

It is curious how the debate has moved on since the first edition of this book was written in 1988. Everywhere human resourcing is on managers' lips. And it is interesting that human resourcing has been adopted with such enthusiasm by so many line managers, particularly Chief Executives. Indeed, many successful HR strategies seem to depend more on the Chief Executive than on the personnel department as their intellectual driving force.

HR is concerned with the management of people at work and to that extent has the same purpose as personnel management. There are, however, fundamental differences, often seeming trivial at first sight but ultimately having a crucial effect. It is true that in the 1980s it was less possible to be sure whether human resourcing was something essentially different or simply the latest management fad. Now the position is clear.

Is HR different from personnel management?

In all of its aspects, HR gathers from what went before. Although credited with being new, the term has been around for many years. For example, the American *Journal of Human Resource Management* was, in 1994, in its 34th year of publication. If personnel managers do not demonstrate their role as inheritors of the HR mantle, others will do so, with personnel departments left simply to administer routine personnel practice.

It is, of course, possible that HR will be absorbed into and change people's perception of what personnel management is about. In the

1

US, Japan, and UK (and, to a lesser extent, Continental Europe) personnel management is already moving to accommodate HR. In the UK, the process may be slow. However, the acute observer will have noted that the IPM journal, *Personnel Management*, added to its title in 1988 (without debate or explanation among the Institute's members) the words 'the journal for human resource specialists'. This piece of insurance will, if necessary, allow the journal to emphasize one at the expense of the other as time progresses. The impact of HR in the UK can perhaps be monitored over time by any changes in print size in the journal's title and subtitle!

HR was, in the 1980s, regarded by some observers and personnel managers as just another name for 'personnel management'. Is it simply old wine in new bottles? As this book will show, there is probably more to it than that. However, even if the judgement of history is that HR was 'just another fad', that would not necessarily discredit what is taking place. There is nothing wrong with reshaping and remarketing a product, and personnel professionals should not apologize for taking a fresh look at their job.

HR emphasizes people as a key resource, from which flows the ultimate strength or weakness of the organization. It is, of course, possible to think and act in these terms in traditional personnel management practices and there are no doubt organizations which do so. Yet there are probably more cases in which personnel professionals consider that insufficient attention is paid to HR problems and their solutions. For them, the new label (the product reshape/relaunch) may help overcome internal organizational barriers.

What are the roots of HR?

Some of the threads of HR that will be described in this text can probably be traced back to the days of Robert Owen who, in the period from 1820 to 1850, became an influential utopian socialist, seeing individual progress as linked to commercial success. Similar themes can be seen in the efforts described by Elton Mayo at the Hawthorne works of the Western Electric Company in the USA. Further significant contributions can be found in the observations of Abraham Maslow. Although both Mayo and Maslow are often associated with the so-called 'behavioural science movement' of the 1960s, it seems to be forgotten that their research goes back much earlier. Mayo commenced his Hawthorne studies in 1931 and reported in 1936 and Maslow's 'Hierarchy of Needs' was first published in 1943 (Maslow 1943).

Drucker (Drucker 1955) built on these foundations, seeing the need for creative leadership and clear goal setting as a spur to commitment and a creative employee contribution. Douglas McGregor (McGregor 1960) emphasized the need to see people management as an integral part of the management of the organization as a whole. Both McGregor and Drucker expressed contempt for what they saw as the 'personnel firefighters' who relied on personnel techniques, manuals and forms to manage people at work. McGregor also wanted personnel professionals to persuade management to examine their beliefs and assumptions about work and why people work. Furthermore, he wanted managers to recognize the consequences of their behaviour towards their people.

Contributors such as Argyris (Argyris 1964) and Herzberg (Herzberg 1966) broke new ground in the 1960s. The importance of planning and then integrating personnel strategies within a coherent framework was emphasized, and they highlighted the need to earn employee commitment by deliberate managerial action. However, many practitioners found the somewhat idealistic tone of their work difficult to apply in the cut-and-thrust environment of the period up to 1973.

One strand of the behavioural sciences provided impetus for the 'organizational development' (OD) movement of the 1960s. Walter Bennis (Bennis 1959) saw OD as a new concept of power, based on collaboration and reason rather than coercion and threat. Edward Schein (Schein 1970) thought of OD as managing the culture of the organization. Both considered organizational behaviour (OB) a central aspect of the personnel manager's efforts.

In the 1970s, work to improve the application of planning and a strategic framework to personnel management found expression in 'manpower planning'. The concept was introduced partly to counter what was seen as a woolly and undisciplined approach to 'people problems' in organizations. The UK Institute of Manpower Studies (IMS) remains one of its key exponents, although it often prefers to use the more general-sounding term 'manpower management' (Bennison and Casson 1984) which reflects its growing and widening role. In the US and Europe, the concept was used extensively, although without the wide-ranging, all-embracing flavour that has occasionally been attributed to it in the UK. The recognition that planning, technology and information had a role in people management was a significant step forward, although manpower planning, like OD, has sometimes been criticized as being too theoretical.

The developing theoretical framework of human resourcing is shown in Figure 1.1, which demonstrates the gradual emergence of

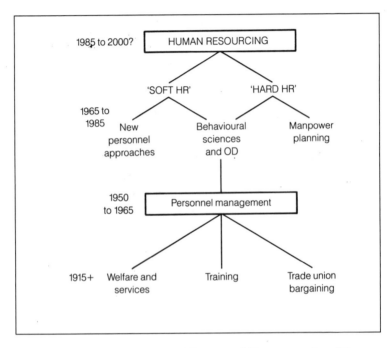

Figure 1.1 The Development of Personnel Management and Human Resourcing

a 'culture focus' to managing people at work. There is also the need felt by personnel people to overcome the tensions and contradictions within their jobs. HR, with its emphasis on people and quality, holds out the prospect of a neat and welcome solution to the people-production paradox – the prospect of creative togetherness to replace previous strains and conflicts.

Empirical experience of excellence

It was apparent throughout much of the period up to the 1980s that the HR approach had strong theoretical roots. Two more conditions were required for the interest to develop further. First, it was essential that organizations identified a need for a people-centred approach. Second, the theoretical framework had to be seen in practical operation since, given the pace of change, strategic fixed plans would never be relevant for very long.

This led to the twin pillars of the modern organization:

- creativity and flexibility to meet the unforeseen
- customer service and the need for quality.

The expression of this development came in the seminal text *In Search of Excellence* (Peters and Waterman 1982). New words appeared in the personnel literature: quality, service, the customer, creativity, objectives, trust, leadership, integrity. These were to be the new language, summed up by the term 'excellence'. However, this objective could not be fulfilled without the support and participation of the workforce. The achievement of such excellence would be by a new approach to managing people at work – human resource management.

Idealistic fervour

One objective of this text is to avoid the undisciplined idealism that can be found elsewhere. It probably does not help to emulate the behavioural scientists of the 1960s (or Maslow much earlier) and display an almost religious zeal about HR in the organization. The aim is always to relate to the organization and its needs. HR is not proposed as an end in itself, but as a means of achieving the organization's objectives. Bonus schemes, for example, may not be the 'HR way' of paying a production line worker, but it is better to use a bonus scheme than to expect performance and output to improve or be maintained solely by expressions of hope. There may well be environments where the implementation of some aspects of a desired HR plan is not possible because the culture does not allow it and culture change is not feasible, or because the manager can find no way to proceed which does not threaten the company. This latter point deserves clarification. HR, like personnel management, is about selecting, rewarding and developing people *to enable the organization to achieve its goals.* Of course, the employees' commitment is conditional and dependent on the opportunities for fulfilment that the company can provide.

Unitary v. pluralistic frameworks

In the US and Japan, some companies at least (e.g. IBM, Hewlett Packard and Sony) appear to adopt a unitary approach to HR – all employees *have* to support the organization and its aims. The British and perhaps the other Europeans appear to adopt a more pluralistic approach to personnel management, which sees the organization as a coalition of often competing interests. Here is a contrast between traditional personnel management and HR – although British companies are now beginning to entertain a unitary frame of reference.

This is particularly noticeable in the tendency to marginalize the role of the trade unions. Storey makes a distinction between 'hard' and 'soft' HR. The hard focuses on planning and control; and the soft – perhaps 'business-humane' is a better term – focuses on communication, leadership and commitment. The problem is that these may be descriptions of the differences between the world as it is (personnel management) and as we would like it to be (human resourcing). Only when fully tested in new environments will the true value of HR be known.

Principles of a human resources strategy

A unity of purpose

What, therefore, are the essential features of the development of a human resources strategy? The first is a recognition of a *unity of purpose* between the employee and the employer to replace the pluralist approach that has previously held sway. The 'employer' is no longer seen as an enemy by the 'employee'. There is a growing recognition that we rise or fall together. Social changes have helped this development as the owner-manager has become a rarer breed. Many 'employers' are themselves 'employees'. Of course, national and international pressures on business mean that the creation and maintenance of lean, people-centred, volume organizations will not be easy. Tough decisions still have to be taken and sometimes those decisions hurt.

Change is normal

A second essential recognition in an HR strategy is that people should not become the victims of change. If people fear change they will resist it. So a climate has to be created in which change is accepted as a normal part of working in an organization. Not even as 'inevitable' – for although it is, the word gives the impression of its being unwelcome and of people having to come to terms with it. A situation has to be created where people *welcome* change. Therefore the underlying causes of resistance have to be understood and catered for. Many of these reasons can be summed up in one word – incompetence. Change makes people's skills redundant, thus making them incompetent.

It is not often realized how devastating change can be to competence. This, in turn, not only affects a person's self-respect but, more to the point, affects job security. If you are incompetent you will not be required. In order, therefore, to prevent or reduce the likelihood of people becoming the victims of change, we must develop strategies that lessen that likelihood (for example through continuous learning) or give people generous £ (or whatever) shaped exits.

The learning organization

The chief way to prevent people becoming outdated is to continually update their skills. Chapter 3 sets this out in more detail but the fundamental point is that employees come to accept a 'lifetime of learning' in a 'learning organization'. This is not solely intended to keep their skills up to date but also allows the adoption through training of new techniques by people who are receptive. This continuity of learning is important, partly because one piece of know-

ledge makes learning the rest easier, but also because if a person
stops for any length of time it becomes difficult or impossible to
restart the motor. Many people give up in their 40s and 50s 'because
you cannot teach an old dog new tricks'. This only happens because
they gave up learning a long while before. In this changing world,
people must be willing for their own sakes to go on learning, and the
business must create the environment in which continuous learning
can take place. (This is discussed more fully in Chapter 3.)

Reward management

This emphasis on learning and skills brings us neatly to the rest area
for an HR strategy. The old scales and annual increments so
beloved of collectivist employer/union structures will become a
thing of the past (particularly if inflation is held in check). Reward
management strategies have to be explored and developed that find
new ways of measuring and then paying for performance. The
1980s was marked in the UK by a relatively homogeneous pay
market and compressed differentials. There was little reward for
gaining new skills in this environment. An HR reward strategy has
to do its best to maximize the rewards for performance and skill
acquisition and other key organizational aims. But some awkward
questions remain unanswered: for example, the durability of performance-related pay schemes (Chapter 7) and whether they should
be individually or group based. No reward solution is likely to stay
right for long, and so an HR strategy based on flexible remuneration
policies is the answer, perhaps backed by a broad pay points system
(discussed in Chapter 7).

Committed employees

The creation of a unitary framework will only be possible if
employees believe that they *share common objectives with the
organization* and therefore have a sense of commitment to it. It is
here that an HR department has much to say. Many destructive
ways of behaving need changing. The recognition of the proper role
of the team leader ('supervisor' in the old language) is a case in
point – for example by allowing the team leader to ring a prospec-
tive employee up at home to make a provisional job offer.

There are other crucial developments of which communications is one. The HR strategy must include *rapid, up-to-date briefing processes.* If people are to be committed they must be told what is going on. This relates closely to the need to develop mutual trust so that problems can be shared and performance needs and weaknesses faced and resolved. (This is discussed more fully in Chapter 8.)

Equal opportunities

An HR organization is an *equal opportunity organization.* How can an organization develop trust if some of its members are discriminated against? At the same time, there is pressure to ensure that the best possible use is made of people's skills, and this is not possible if the abilities of a section of the population or workforce are ignored or under-utilized. Therefore, an HR strategy will consider the development of 'family-friendly' policies (and the costs and benefits of implementing them). Equal opportunity policies also entail a close look at possible insidious discrimination. There are external bodies with which it is possible to become associated, such as Opportunity 2000 which aims to develop and widen the perceived role of women. These can give an organization public standing on such issues – which can be useful in driving home the same issues within the company. (This is discussed more fully in Chapter 10.)

Motivation .

There are many ways in which employers can successfully motivate employees. Many, however, are transitory in their effect. For example, it is possible to motivate employees to have good attendance at work by the payment of an attendance bonus, but it is unlikely to have a beneficial effect beyond a year or two. After that, conflict will arise based on a gradually increasing perception of unfairness due to the implied threat of penalizing people who are ill. HR strategy is about policies that last longer than a year or two. Therefore the search will be for policies that attract people to work through their social and psychological contracts not just through a concentration on narrow interpretations of financial and legal contracts. (This is discussed more fully in Chapters 11 and 12.)

De-layering and empowerment/flexibility

Any HR strategy will seek to move away from the bureaucracy and lack of innovation that stops the growth and development of many organizations. One key way of achieving this is by reducing the number of levels in the hierarchy. This results in decisions being made more quickly on the occasions that they must be referred to higher levels of authority because of the size, cost or potential impact of the project.

However, one feature of an HR organization is to encourage *decision taking at as low a level as possible* in the organization. This, in turn, leads to many other important points. If the policy is to be successful, people must be flexible in their jobs. They cannot be narrowly confined by restrictive practices and job descriptions (or job restrictions!). At the same time, employees must continuously educate themselves to update, widen and change their skills.

These changes (decentralized authority, de-layered organization, flexibility and learning/education) all lead to 'empowerment'. I take this word to mean allowing employees to be responsible for their own areas of work and not to have to wait for the approval of some senior for every minor decision. (These matters are discussed in Chapters 4, 5, 6 and 15.)

Leadership

A feature of western business is that it is over-managed and under-led. This relates to the areas mentioned above (de-layering and empowerment) but much of it revolves around a proper understanding of power. Power as a concept is much maligned but it needs to be thought about. Who has it or who should not have it; what should be added and what should be taken away. Human resourcing is about how people can be successfully managed in an organization to achieve the aims of that organization. To achieve anything yourself, or to work out how you will influence someone or yourself be influenced, requires power and an understanding of it. Empowerment is itself a derivative of power, referring to the increasing likelihood of action being taken by an individual without further hierarchical reference. So power is central to the debate about HR, and a proper understanding of *leadership* is one of the more benign yet positive aspects of power. (This is discussed in Chapter 14.)

Many organizations have to deal with the problem of trade unions who have, perhaps over many years, fought an adversarial struggle with managers who held employees in low esteem. Getting out of the negative bind is not an easy prospect, particularly if individuals come laden with the baggage of history. The managers may be able to deal with the problem by removing those that do not fit the new culture and cannot change to cope. The problem with trade unionists may be more intractable. Most people can, however, be persuaded to see that change is taking place and will respond positively. Many organizations will find the trade unions are only too ready to embrace these aspects of an HR culture.

Management attitudes and change

All this implies a significant change in culture from traditional 'personnel management', and an important starting point for an HR strategy is the need for a *change programme*.

A change programme will involve the organization in coming to terms with its managerial style and the implications of that style. It may be very difficult to persuade a manager that, for example, the alienated, unhelpful workforce is due to the low trust that has been placed in it by the management, perhaps over many years.

However, even if acceptance of managerial responsibility is achieved, change is not easy. If an aggressive management style, backed up by rigorous policing and controls, is simply 'switched off', there is more than a chance that, for a period at least, abuse by employees will be rife. An organization may be able to wait for the changed policies to take effect, but there will be many organizations that financially or politically cannot afford the risk.

If the organization works well and is successful and profitable, the manager will rightly be wary of change that may impair rather than improve effectiveness. These two difficulties (employee attitudes to change and the risk of failure) explain why many of the companies that have managed to make significant achievements did so from a position of near disaster. Staring Armageddon in the face can concentrate the attention of managers and employees, which facilitates a cultural break with the past and the ushering in of a new era. For the same reason, many companies operating within an HR framework are on 'greenfield' sites. They build the desired culture completely from new, even though they behave in their old ways at their other locations!

Failing the mission

There is another difficulty that needs addressing. What happens when the organization's mission ('to be the best', for example) is not achieved? For a while it may be possible to re-package and redouble efforts. But the mission might wear thin over the years and then employees could become cynical about the process as failure breeds disappointment. This would be particularly galling if an organization was disintegrating because of factors outside its control: raw material problems, government tax regimes, economic recession and so on. The organization needs to be sure that the *HR environment is durable* and can overcome such reverses. One solution is to temper the mission statement to an expression of general aims and leave measurement and quantification to objective setting.

The organization as the centre

It is also worth touching on another basic problem. HR in all its aspects sees *the organization as the purpose.* Everything is done to achieve the corporate mission. Employee development may be laudable and it may be significant, but it is not altruistic – the plans are established and carried out because they benefit the organization. There will be those for whom the emphasis on the common interest between the employer and the employed is unacceptable. There are also those who believe that there are limits to the extent of personal fulfilment that can be achieved in an economic or working environment.

The Chief Executive

One advantage of limited horizons is that the modest aspirant can hope to achieve them within their own sphere of accountability. Since HR is based on questioning and rebuilding the culture and moulding *every* employee plan, it requires involvement at the highest levels of power in the organization. It is very interesting that many well-known HR strategies have been the brain-children of the Chief Executive.

This poses two problems for the personnel function. First, if the Chief Executive cannot be persuaded, progress is going to be limited. It is very difficult to conceive of a company-wide HR plan working for one function of an organization, while an adjacent department still uses traditional personnel methods.

Second, given the support of the Chief Executive, there may well be question as to whether the personnel department has any significant contribution to make in the formulation and implementation of an HR plan. The personnel function has been warned (Purcell 1985 and Fowler 1987): the Chief Executive may be saying that they are not delivering the goods of contributing usefully to strategic thinking about people. If that idea were to gain ground, then HR would develop as a separate corporate approach to planning organization behaviour (OB). The personnel function would then be just the provider of the forms, procedures and techniques – the operational details of someone else's strategy, ready for outsourcing when the moment arrived.

The remainder of this text assumes that the HR role should and will properly fall on the shoulders of the HR/personnel function as the key adviser in this domain to the Chief Executive and the Board, of which the 'HR Director' is a member.

Chapter 2

Customers and Quality – Above All Else

> Management literature is replete with discussion about 'customers' and its bedfellow 'quality'. Why is this the case? (Bayley 1987)

Customers have always existed; what manager in the 1950s would not have considered his products of the highest quality or would have admitted to not serving the customer? Yet judging by the impact of the customer/quality message, important developments appear to be taking place. Wickens has made great play of this in his 'tripod of success' (Wickens 1988) shown in Figure 2.1.

Satisfying demand

There was, said Peters (IMI Conference 1987), such a pent-up demand among the general population after 15 years of depression and 5 years of war that from 1945 manufacturers could sell anything. This phenomenon of unsatisfied demand has been mirrored in the relatively closed Eastern European economies. Shoppers there are required to accept goods that Western or affluent Asian buyers would not buy. The latter would never have to return goods of such poor quality because they would not buy them in the first place. Therefore in what are relatively accessible Western and Far Eastern markets, customers are able to choose their purchases with care. Consequently, suppliers have to prepare their products more carefully and aim them more accurately at their potential market. There is, of course, another factor: when a customer has experienced

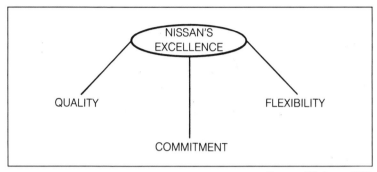

Figure 2.1   The Nissan Tripod   Source: Wickens 1988

quality goods or service, there is no going back. Poor-quality goods or services will be rejected.

Organizational perceptions of quality

Perhaps more important however was the significant intervention of the Oriental (particularly Japanese) manufacturers. Traditional Western attitudes to quality were based on the assumption that if you performed a number of tasks in producing goods then a proportion of the finished product would not work. That this attitude actually legitimized and therefore encouraged faults was ignored. The Japanese are proof that cultural value systems are crucial in the consideration of quality products and service.

The Western cultural value system was proved to be wrong. The Japanese stressed the 'zero defect' product. Customers would be gained by being given what they wanted. Design, manufacture, assembly, distribution and selling would all focus on the search for perfection in the goods or services offered.

Quality – someone else's problem

Some readers might ask why there is a chapter on customers and quality in a book on personnel. In fact personnel management's role in service has been stressed before (Bayley 1987). This is a reflection of the personnel department's belief that people (customers and employees) and quality are the job of the whole organization, not just part of it. Many companies have employed 'quality control inspectors' to supervise and maintain quality. But this misses the real issue of why quality was not *built in* to the product or service in the first place. Indeed the issue becomes deeper even than that, for it is also a question of *designing* quality into the product before production even starts. The very use of quality controllers, supervisors, inspectors, work study officers and so on reinforces a basic cultural view that 'quality is not part of my job' and that quality control is handled by the specialists.

Arguments were centred on production and cost, and quality and customers were sacrificed in the process. This is not to say that production schedules, budgets, costs and the rest are not crucially important. The cultural change implied by human resourcing is that if the needs of employees, customers and quality are met, everything else will fall naturally into place. For example, if the customer will not pay the product price then that implies that there is something wrong with the price being charged for the quality or level of service. The problem may therefore be one of productivity or cost control. The point is that satisfying the needs of the employee is the way in which quality is maintained, customers are served and costs are controlled. The importance of employees underlines the need for human resources planning for employee commitment, which again has been the subject of debate (Martin and Nicholls 1988) and is discussed in Chapter 11.

Value systems

References to 'values' and 'value systems' were appearing in the late 1960s and 1970s in personnel literature. This was an early recognition of the importance of commitment and *shared* values in achieving organizational change. This was the period of organizational development (OD). The problem was that the proponents of OD seemed somewhat too evangelical for many managers – OD seemed to be changing the function of the organization from a concern with business to a concern with philosophy. The 'customer culture' has provided the answer. The value system language of the 1960s and 1970s suddenly makes sense to managers who know about the customer-quality approach and can readily relate to it as

good business practice. Managers who were cynical about the pro-
selytizing of the OD consultants in the 1970s can readily relate to
the hard-headed business sense of the customer-quality focus. The
'values' thinking has been combined with a line manager's hard-
nosed commercial desire to sell a product or service.
The combination in full swing is awesomely successful, as the
Japanese have shown. This combination, 'total quality management', has a powerful appeal across three key areas of concern.

1 It has *an attractive external image* which is good for business and
assures potential customers.
2 It has a *wide appeal to the senior executive team*, from whatever
background they might come, who can readily relate to it.
3 *Internally* it is a clarion call that *employees* can respond to.

Job satisfaction

The emphasis on customers had one other effect that may not
always be obvious and was probably not envisaged. One problem
for personnel managers has always been how employees can be
fulfilled in repetitive or unpleasant jobs. This search for job satisfaction and job enrichment led to much discussion and literature
(Harper 1987). The search was only partially successful. Many jobs
are now recognized to be intrinsically tedious, dirty or otherwise
unpopular. The ability of people to confound the theorists led to
job satisfaction studies which found (Gowler 1974, Mayo 1933,
Harper 1987) that different people responded differently to the
same type of work. What one employee found exciting another did
not and vice versa. There was also the inevitable discovery that the
organization of work for the benefit of employees might not make
much sense from an economic/cost point of view. In the long run
there always had to be a balance between people and economy –
one could never be sacrificed to the other.

Context of work

One realization that emerged from the 'job satisfaction movement'
was the importance of work *context* over work *content* arising from

the work of contingency theorists (eg Fiedler 1974), who argued that satisfaction depended on circumstances (context) as much as on job content. In simple terms, the idea underpinning job satisfaction and job enrichment was that if jobs could be made more satisfying then commitment would increase, labour turnover reduce and so on. This was an attempt to apply Maslow's hierarchy of needs in practice. As referred to above, altering work content proved difficult and varying human perceptions meant that not everyone approved anyway.

At the same time, some researchers mused over the apparent contradiction that a Chief Executive, who at the office would have found clerical or, even worse, manual work demeaning (and the justification for a constructive dismissal claim!), was nevertheless quite happy to shift manure and dig onion beds at home during the weekend! The explanation was that the dissatisfaction at the office came not from the work itself but from the *context* in which it was carried out.

The search for job satisfaction would only ever be partially successful for the key issue was how the work was seen by colleagues, superiors and subordinates. It perhaps follows from this that an emphasis on context rather than content is the key to job satisfaction. The focus on customers and quality could provide the framework for employees to make personal sense, at a human level, of what they are doing. No longer a cog in a huge wheel, each employee is free to put as much of her or himself into customer care and quality as she or he sees fit.

Manufacturing and service

Coming to terms with customers and quality is of course not without its problems. In the manufacturing sector, 'total quality' has an obvious appeal. The introduction of quality circles was most prevalent in manufacturing. The attraction was obvious – costs were reduced while higher quality meant higher prices. Every reduction in cost brought increased revenue. If the results had not been there for everyone to see, it would not have been believed. Certainly the books would not have sold! As it was, quality circles were, for a while, good business for both consultants and authors (Collard and Dale 1985).

Service industries, however, have not found customer care and quality so easy to achieve. Perhaps the most important point is that service work involves a greater degree of person-to-person interchange, and where people relate things will go wrong. There is also the problem of the infinite variety of customer expectations as to what constitutes 'good' service. Finally, customer expectations appear to be rising. For service sectors the lack of a concrete product means that those expectations are less structured than they would be in the manufacturing sector.

The main problem for the service sector is reliance on humans to give the service itself. It is not like buying a motor car or hi-fi where the service and quality is built into the product and passed on in that way. In the service sector, improved service can require an investment in systems and people that increases costs. The need to control costs requires a realistic strategy to focus on the requirements of the specific customers to be served. This identification of and assault on specified market segments, following analysis and market research, provides the best chance of maximizing service and quality at an affordable cost. Of course, customers may well be willing to pay the price for increased personal service and there are signs that this is the case. It is also apparent that customers will accept the limitations imposed by the level of service they are paying for. However, there is one overriding principle – when the point of contact is reached, the customer expects (and deserves) courtesy and concern – a quality service. Needless to say, no amount of courtesy or explanation will make up for a bad product. Quality in the back-up service but not in the product is as useless as the reverse.

British Airways is reported (Martin and Nicholls 1988) as having met and dealt with this problem of market segmentation and identification. The reference above includes the following example by Michael Thomas.

In 1983 British Airways, in the course of its efforts to recapture a value-added image, intensified its market research, trying to establish exactly what it was that made passengers elect to fly a particular airline again – repeat purchase being a very significant factor in this industry's revenue.

Through a rather more imaginative research approach than previously adopted, the airline identified a number of salient features of service for its major passenger segments. For relatively inexperienced VFR passengers (visiting friends and relations), anxiety reduction was paramount; for holiday-makers glamour, champagne and excitement were the key; while for the experienced and perhaps jaundiced business traveller on short hauls the needs were described as 'rational' – a timely arrival, special communication facilities in the event of unavoidable delays and so on.

This research certainly helped in the development of a largely successful strategy and clearly pointed to a need to promote the facets of sympathy and courtesy – the elements of the well-publicized 'putting people first' campaign. But sophisticated though the research was, it failed to identify one potentially important feature for the last passenger segment, the business traveller. For in the spring of 1983 a small airline called British Midland introduced the breakfast sausage to early-morning internal flights and bleary-eyed businessmen switched carriers in their thousands. The supposed rationality of business travellers did, of course, demand timeliness and facilities, but the added value was the sausage – the cattle-truck 'shuttle' had been displaced. To BA's credit, it managed within months to launch the super shuttle, complete with breakfast, and its dominance was re-established.

The moral of this story is not that BA got it wrong – to err is human – but rather that some flair is required in establishing exactly what the important features are, in identifying the 'sausage factor' and in being sufficiently nimble to provide it quickly.

Communicating the customer–quality message

The question of communication is dealt with in more detail in Chapter 8. At this stage it is important to stress the importance of getting the customer–quality message across to employees. There are a number of vital ingredients to any such process, as shown in Figure 2.2.

First, it is essential to have top *management support*. The customer–quality message cannot be driven home by personnel departments or even by the support departments. The support must come from those who have the direct responsibility and the power to make changes.

Secondly, the *message must be simple*. The KISS approach (Keep It Simple, Stupid!) has much to commend it. This is the area where brevity and conciseness in employee communications has its place.

Management Support
Keep the Message Simple (KISS)
Objectives Must be Achievable and Achieved
Discuss Conflicts/Contradictions Openly
Build Customer Care into Company Training Programmes
Involve Employees
Commitment comes from Co-operation not Coercion
A Focus of Attention on Employees

Figure 2.2   Vital Ingredients in Communicating the Customer–Quality Message

Mission statements have been maligned, but in terms of providing a simple summary of what the organization is trying to achieve they can claim to be successful (Martin and Nicholls 1988).

Thirdly, the objective must be tough, achievable and *achieved*. The communication strategy will quickly fall into disrepute if there are no internal or external signs of success.

Fourthly, conflicts and contradictions must be *discussed openly*. A senior line manager may consider cost-cutting an imperative, but such an approach may be perceived by employees as harming the achievement of customer care and quality levels.

Fifthly, customer care and quality must be built into *training and development* programmes. These may be aimed at simply getting the message across, but will more likely have specific training and behaviour-channelling aims. Employees have to be persuaded that customers and quality are important and then discover for themselves how to achieve it.

Sixthly, practical *employee involvement* is likely to bring the commitment that is needed. Some kind of management-motivated and structured environment is necessary to enable employees to look at customer-quality issues and see how improvements might be made. Quality circles have been the most significant and popular attempt to achieve this end and they have been successful for many organizations (Collard and Dale 1985). There should, however, be a note of caution. Quality circles depend for their success on a set of particular circumstances. These include a belief in people, a concern for customers and quality, a recognition of the importance of commitment, the need for employee involvement and so on. It is hardly likely that quality circles will flourish without these pre-requisites. It is highly probable that quality circles are the result of and not the cause of a company's concern for the customer–quality–employee triumvirate. It is interesting to note that those companies which appear to have succeeded with quality circles (or their deriva-tives) such as Black and Decker, IBM and Hewlett Packard, have, it is said, for a long time believed in the importance of customers, quality and employee involvement.

Finally, there is a fundamental need to recognize that quality comes from *commitment and co-operation* and not coercion. It is perhaps possible to reduce costs and improve productivity by force but it is unlikely that customer care and quality will emerge by force and management edict. For this reason, the customer–quality focus requires the third aspect, *employees*, in order to be achieved. In turn this requires a recognition of a need for many organizations to change the way that personnel management is practised. This rec-ognition of a new 'people' strategy and the need to plan to achieve it, are the central themes and purposes of human resource planning. Success in organizations depends on the achievement of these strategies. It is interesting to reflect on the attributes of successful organizations as defined by Peters and Waterman (1982). This is summarized in Figure 2.3 and argues the importance of customers, quality and people among other aspects.

Customer care programme

It is essential to link the whole process together in the form of a customer care programme. This will include getting top manage-ment support, setting objectives, analysing the present, publicly, establishing criteria for success and undertaking employee training and development. A typical programme was given in the IPM's 'Factsheet' series and is reproduced in Figure 2.4 (p. 26).

The programme can and perhaps should be supported by incen-tives and backed up by internal or external consultants. Of course its success must be measured. Above all, the organization must be on guard against superficiality. There must be many programmes that have failed because the fundamental shifts in attitude either towards or by employees have not been made.

Peters and Waterman's survey of successful, continuously innovative companies in the USA suggested to them that such companies displayed eight attributes:

1. **A closeness to customers.** They provide quality, service and reliability but they also listen to their customers and often receive ideas for new and improved products from them.

2. **Productivity though people.** They treat rank and file staff as the source of quality and productivity gain; this implies a policy or style which respects the individual as a person.

3. **A bias for action.** They pay great attention to analysis and to the need to think out courses of action but are not inhibited from acting by pandering to this need. Action is expected to follow analysis – and quickly.

4. **Autonony and entrepreneurship.** They foster many 'leaders' at all levels of the organization, encouraging people to innovate and see their innovations through. Staff are not kept on a short rein, which inhibits them, but held together in loose networks of relationships.

5. **Hands-on, value-driven.** They maintain close contacts between the members of the organization, to foster the growth of 'culture', whose values all members of staff share.

6. **Stick to the knitting.** These companies stick close to the business they know; they do not usually seek to become conglomerates in which units are disparate and non-complementary.

7. **Simple form, lean staff.** The structure of these organizations is generally elegantly simple and their headquarters staff is kept small in size. Matrix organizations are generally avoided.

8. **Simultaneous loose-tight properties.** These companies display apparent paradoxes: they are centralized and decentralized; they have central controls and divisional automony. The norms of the culture are relied on to hold the whole together.

In summary, these companies showed themselves committed to people (whether customers or employees) and to action (to improve productivity, quality or service). They expected a professional approach from everyone concerned and respected and rewarded those who provided it. They rejected the idea that any problem needed long investigation and a report before any action could be contemplated; they looked for rapid action, accepting that this would produce mistakes which could nevertheless be tolerated.

Source: Peters and Waterman 1982

Figure 2.3   Attributes of Successful Organizations

Total Quality programmes

Identifiable as a separate management tool through the seminal work of W. Edwards Deming, (a founder of TQM and an American in Japan!) after the war, Total Quality and its derivatives took some time before they became recognized in the Euro-American arena. TQM is the gospel of focusing everyone in the organization on the customer. As it makes an increasing impact within European companies, it seems to be assuming the status of a standard business practice rather than being another passing management fad. This has been underlined by the founding, in December 1993, of the British Quality Foundation (BQF) under ICI Chairman Sir Denys Henderson. The foundation has the strong moral support of Michael Heseltine and a number of heavyweight companies such as British Gas, British Telecom, ICL and Texas Instruments. There is a broadening of activity using such techniques as 'continuous process improvement', 'just-in-time manufacturing', 'statistical process control', as well as related areas such as teamwork, employee participation and benchmarking (Conference Board 1994).

A typical TQ programme seeks to create problem-solving teams that will maximize organizational competitiveness, and various devices to achieve this have been prepared. There are now many preparatory methods available, but perhaps most encouraging are the programmes available from the BQF.

Summary

Customers and quality, together with employees, make up the key components of many organizations. The traditional problems of quality, costs and customer perceptions have to be addressed, and there is a danger of treating quality as 'someone's else's' job. The customer–quality focus must be recognized as part of the company's value system. Work *context* as opposed to work *content* can be vitally important as an alternative approach to job enrichment and job satisfaction. There must be a structured, thought-out and relevant customer care and quality programme, and the organization should guard against superficiality and consequent failure. The importance of employee participation rather than management coercion must be stressed. With participation might come employee commitment and teamwork, and in this way quality can emerge in the organization; but this will only happen if a complete human resource strategy is worked out and its implementation is planned with care and attention to detail.

Step one is to decide the objectives and structure of the programme. It is at this stage that the whole management team needs to commit itself to any changes in policy, such as a new approach to compensation.

Step two is an audit of the current situation. It is common to conduct two attitude surveys, one covering employees (with such questions as 'What would a customer find most unsettling about doing business with me?') and the second covering customers.

Step three is a series of planning workshops at which the procedures for the programme are discussed and agreed. These workshops can develop into team-building exercises and they can also point up causes of frustration for which straightforward remedies are available, ranging from the way work is organized or problems with equipment, such as uncomfortable chairs or inadequate lighting. (An intrinsic part of customer care is employee care.)

Step four is the stage at which policies and objectives are defined and put into action and it is here that the personnel department is likely to become particularly involved. An example of the kind of change that might need to be introduced is to revise recruitment criteria so that customer-service orientation becomes a requirement for all jobs, rather than simply for those jobs that involve direct contact with customers.

Step five is an internal publicity campaign to prepare the ground for the training programme. Although this is normally the responsibility of the public relations or personnel department, this is a marketing activity and needs to be approached as seriously as the organization approaches its external marketing. It can involve many different types of medium – newsletters, company magazines and newspapers, bulletins from the chief executive, video presentations, roadshows etc. The aim is to make the programme sound so exciting and interesting that employees would be prepared, if need be, to give up their own time to take part.

At the same time the organization should be reviewing its communication system, since this will play a vital role in maintaining the impetus once the initial training sessions have been completed.

Step six marks the start of the actual training. There are two main schools of thought as to how this should be structured. The first holds that employees should be divided into 'streams', with separate sessions for managers, supervisors etc; the second favours the adoption of 'vertical slicing' with all levels of staff attending the same courses.

The case for 'streaming' is strengthened if different messages need to be got through to different levels of management. It is also argued that, if managers are put through customer care training first and begin acting on what they have learned, that will reinforce the subsequent training for those they are managing.

The advantage of 'vertical slicing' is that it gives staff who are not in regular contact with customers a better chance to see their job in the context of the total picture.

Whatever approach is adopted the aim always has to be to enable staff to see their job as part of a whole and to understand the contribution made by others in the organization. This has formed a specific phase of the British Airways programme; in its 'A day in the life' sessions, each employee experiences what is involved in every aspect of airline service, from baggage-handling to having a go on a flight simulator. According to the airlines, this has 'resulted in an identification of staff with company goals and a feeling from each person that they are "British Airways"'.

Pizza Hut's Director of Human Resources, Angie Risley, stresses that employees should be given simple messages and that should not be a problem if clear objectives have been established in advance.

Some programmes resort to using a 'new language' with the aim of giving more impact to the basic, simple message. One of the best-known examples is the 'warm fuzzies/cold prickles' approach. This approach can be effective but only if it is appropriate to the audience.

Source: Hogg 1989

Figure 2.4   A Typical Customer Care Programme

Chapter 3

Development, Training and Education

Education and training – a crucial factor

The personnel function has not always attached sufficient importance to education and training. Too often financial problems or the need for savings have led to cuts in the training budget. At the same time, the low esteem in which education and training has been held by some has been mirrored by career aspirations and career paths. The smart money has for too long been on industrial relations and salary administration as a way to progress to the top. It is time for a change.

In human resource planning education, training and development are recognized as fundamental to building quality into the business. Traditional attitudes that view training as something affecting young people are totally inappropriate in an environment of rapid and technological change. The importance of flexibility to HRM is discussed in some detail in Chapter 5. For this type of flexibility to work it is essential that it be underpinned by a commitment to the education and training of all employees.

All employees – a company objective

The availability of education and training to *all* employees is important. Many companies who have an admirable record in training provision nevertheless can be over-restrictive in its application. In many cases it is traditional for most resources to be directed at a narrow range of youth, often male, training. This is particularly the case in the UK and Australia, where numerous covert barriers are in place to deflect older women from training, particularly for the jobs covered by male apprenticeships. (This matter of freedom for women to pursue the career of their choice will be referred to again in Chapter 10.)

Apprenticeship

This concentration on youth training through apprenticeship has been a well-meaning, though failed, attempt to raise standards and generalize training provision. The traditional UK apprenticeship scheme has its roots deeply embedded in an Anglo-Saxon desire for stability through separation and division. The restrictive practices that flowed from this system have been documented frequently (eg Bramham 1988). The most fundamental was the influence the system had on the supply of skilled employees. In practice, if a young person did not become apprenticed in their mid-teens (the age increased as the compulsory school-leaving age rose), there was no chance of becoming a 'craftsman' (note the gender of this crucial word!) later in life. The result of this system was gross inflexibility. Where young people are also separated from the company for between 4 and 6 years during their apprenticeship and treated like schoolchildren, then the position is made worse.

Training and changing needs

From an HR viewpoint a more subtle argument against apprenticeship can be made. The presumption underlying apprenticeship is that all that needs to be learned can be learned before the 21st birthday and after that it is just a matter of experience. This attitude was good enough when nothing much changed and there was little competition. It has no place in a situation where rapid technological changes and advances in techniques can quickly make yesterday's skills irrelevant. This recognition is what makes education and training different in an HR framework. Education and training for employees is a continuous process of personal development. This will range from training within company hours to personal development by the employee out of hours (but perhaps financed by the company).

These criticisms are not new. There have been numerous reports over many years (Cross 1985) making these and similar points. What is new is the recognition that training and development is fundamental to the business and its drive for quality. Education and training is too important to be left only to the producers (the providers of a training service) – it must be corporately directed.

This is why there is such an effort being made to re-establish learning (particularly youth learning) as a top priority. Modern apprenticeships (*PM Plus* December 1993) of the type being sought will only work with the wholehearted support of employers. It is essential that the quality and universal acceptability that was traditionally part of the apprenticeship are integrated with modern needs such as problem solving, teamwork, and interpersonal and IT skills.

One encouraging development in the UK has been the establishment of the 'Investors in People' standard. IiP has been enthusiastically accepted by government and many employers. There are four stages or 'Principles' to the standard:

Principle 1 – Commitment
Principle 2 – Review
Principle 3 – Action
Principle 4 – Evaluation

These stages will include diagnosis and self-diagnosis of the company's strengths and weaknesses often by managers backed up by employee surveys. It is also necessary to produce a portfolio of evidence in preparation for final assessment by TEC staff and their consultant supporters.

With varying degrees of enthusiasm and success TECs (Training and Enterprise Councils) have the task of delivering and maintaining the standards among employers. The standard has within its framework various linkages that provide a good base for much of human resourcing (see Figure 3.1) and therefore the achievement of the standard is entirely consistent with the principles outlined in this text. (Gwent TEC 1993).

It is now recognized that existing frameworks for education and training, in the UK at least, are inappropriate for the task expected.

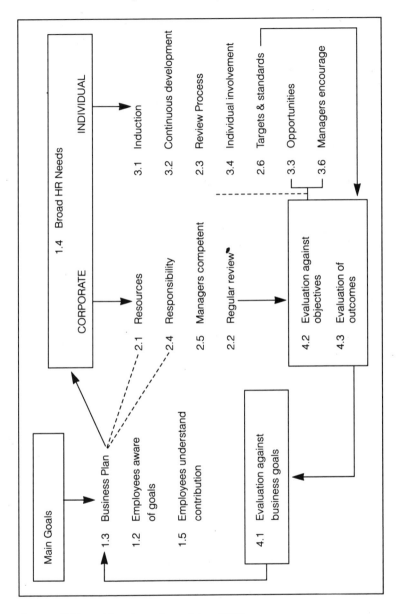

Source: Whitton Meacham Associates 1993.

Figure 3.1   Linkages within IiP standard

The cumbersome advisory and qualification-awarding bodies, institutes and committees are being replaced by a system that puts education and training firmly on the corporate agenda. The National Council for Vocational Qualifications' (NCVQ) (SVQ in Scotland) shows every sign of recognizing and meeting the challenge. If it is successful a more flexible but still rigorous approach to vocational qualifications is in prospect. This will of course entail some rude shocks for managers who for too long have dismissed education and training as a backwater role, seeing it as a handy way of passing a little knowledge on to employees and as a congenial way of spending a couple of days.

This is a big task for HR, and will require careful planning and restructuring of management attitudes to education and training and the external provision of courses. It will also require a reappraisal of how internal training is structured, how courses are managed, and how education and training is managed within the HR function.

Getting resources into education and training

The amount of funding available will clearly affect the amount and quality of education and training that can be undertaken. A major problem arises because of a fundamental mistake by professional educators and trainers. There is a supposition that resources will follow the identification of a need by the producers.

In this respect education and training has to accept the disciplines that apply to other aspects of the company. If the products that are being provided are not wanted by the customer you do not blame the customer! The determination of education and training priorities in the organization should be customer- not producer-led.

This principle is also important in schools. In that case the customers are the parents (as responsible for their children and their education) who are also the resource-generators and therefore have a second reason to be involved. Added to this, industry is a secondary, more distant customer. For this reason the growing involvement of industry in education at school and university is an important foundation-stone that can be built on by an HR approach within the company.

The principle underlying these assumptions is that the *risk-taker/ resource-generator* should take decisions and not the *adviser/*

producer. Producers within education cannot have the discipline that would be imposed by a risk of failure. In education the line of responsibility is too long and diffuse and so the educators have less to lose if the customer fails. Indeed, the situation is made worse because any risk-taking that is involved is of a professional nature. This is, in turn, judged by other professional producers! The opportunities for sterility and inbreeding are obvious and perhaps explain the resistance educators can sometimes express towards any comment or pressure coming from outside.

School and industry liaison

The lack of mutuality between education and training in part explains the mistrust which is common on the part of industry educators. In the 1980s both the UK and the US governments picked up this general feeling, which arose because of the separation of producers, customers and resource-generators. What was wrong was the presumption underlying some thinking that teachers as individuals were somehow deficient professionally. The HR manager would have explained that the place to direct critical attention is the organizational infrastructure. Once that is made answerable and responsive to external influence, individuals will have a clearer knowledge about what is expected of them and can act accordingly. Educators cannot be blamed for establishing their own value systems in education if society's lack of interest has failed to put in place a different perspective. (It is also probable that the educators' perspective was originally approved by society and that society has now moved on and wants and needs a new perspective.)

It is fundamental therefore that resources will follow only where the generator of those resources is committed to the task which is proposed. It should come as no surprise that if the task is not understood it will not be supported. In summary therefore, the extra resources that are required in both in-company and school education will follow only if there is a commitment to education and training in the company and society, and this will occur through sharing and involvement. The planning of this result is central to improving the provision and development of human resources within the company. (CBI 1988)

In the US the Dukakis Boston compacts and magnet schools and, in the UK, training and enterprise councils (TECs) are attempts to rewrite the agenda and make education and training the responsibility of the community and the company, not only of producers. One point of clarification should, however, be added. The above refers to the value systems and objectives of education and training within schools and companies and the level of resources allocated – these are rightly the customers' not the producers' responsibility. This is an involvement at a human resource planning level. At the tactical level, however, the tutor should be free to determine *how* (as opposed to *what*) content will be delivered within the overall framework. The tutor, like any other employee, needs maximum freedom to be creative and adaptive. There should be no interference in delivery unless objectives are not being met in a particular case.

What type of education and training?

Too much of our education and training has failed to do the job expected of it (and here again the UK is at fault). Underlying it has been a reliance on theory and knowledge for its own sake. This is a single and limiting strand of educational thought derived from an obsolete culture (Plato's Greece). It is still defended doggedly by many schools and universities and is mimicked by some in-company training.

There is a preference among some professionals for theory over practice, idealism over reality and, particularly worryingly, old over new wisdoms. This leads to some crass examples of snobbery. A manager in the company will express a total lack of interest in computers but would not dream of showing ignorance about the opening bars of Beethoven's 5th!

The value system has created a situation where knowing rather than doing is at a premium. This preference for knowledge has been reinforced by an examination and in-company testing system which rewards those who can analyse rather than those who have understanding and can integrate knowledge with experience. This in turn leads to a passion for the grading of people through written assessment. This interest in specialism and pure knowledge is necessary for those whose work involves the grasp and development of pure theory. In the company it is damaging.

Doers not knowers – competence-based training

People, the human resources, are the key to a company's success. Planning for their education and training should be based on doing not knowing. This is the principle that underpins the concept of competence-based training. This is a search for a proper blend of teaching and learning which of course embraces knowledge and received wisdom but which emphasizes 'doing' skills and is not constrained by traditional views of what is thought to be of value.

This emphasis on competence will have a futher important result for the planning of human resources in the company. There is still a strong tendency for large numbers of the population to abandon education altogether as soon as they can. (Very large numbers do not even bother to wait until the end of compulsory state schooling.) Competence training with its concentration on performance will convince more employers of the need to give time and commitment to learning new skills.

Competence is based on the possession of skills rather than knowledge. Facts are of limited value without the ability to apply them competently. A fundamental mistake that is often made is to equate knowledge with wisdom. This is made more acute because knowledge wears out while wisdom grows, adapts and creates. Again the driving force of HRM can be seen – rapid and diverse change, much of it technological in nature. Employees must see their role as accepting these challenges for change. This is not to dismiss theory, for it is an essential ingredient which underpins a wider application of skills, but knowledge and theory alone are not enough.

The competence approach is not going to be adopted without some difficulty and heart-searching. It is remarkable how many company training assessments are based on a presumption that knowledge is at a premium. Especially written but also oral examinations are directed to examining the extent to which knowledge has been acquired. A change in attitude is required among examining bodies in the professional and the 'skill' trades. The difficulty of achieving this should not be underestimated. (Try and consider how the competence level of a painting by Turner compared with a Constable might be assessed!)

Learning not teaching

The problem for the trainer/teacher is not underestimated either. A knowledge-based system of education and training places a premium on the transfer of information – *on teaching*. Competence, however, is a question of skills application and understanding – of *learning*. Of course there is teaching for competence as well, but the emphasis is quite different. For competence the individual cannot be a passive receiver of bits of information. The individual is required to participate and discover for her or himself.

Again, this is important in terms of human resource planning. The individual who is allowed to participate in the learning process will have greater commitment to the education and training that is being delivered than might otherwise be the case. This will reinforce the point made earlier: the widening of the base for education and training at school, at college and at work needs to be encouraged.

One further aspect underpinning all competences should be mentioned – the importance of *communication* and particularly *oral skills*. HR recognizes communicative and oral skills as being essential to the business of the future. Organizations will see the leader of a work team as seeking achievement through others. Because of the variety and technological content of jobs, allied with a need to give good service, the individual will be very much alone in deciding how to do the job. This makes it important that the company's general objectives are well communicated by the team leader and consequently understood by the employee.

Competence – the importance of 'on the job training'

For too many people the thought of a training course conjures up visions of some restful and pleasing hotel stay. There will be residential training but, if training in HR is to be a continuous and frequent process, it will not be possible to give it such special treatment. By and large training in an HR environment will take place as closely as possible to that environment. This implies on-the-job or at least on-site training.

The UK government's Training Commission gave the definition of on-the-job training shown in Figure 3.2. That definition was framed as part of a general survey of off-the-job and on-the-job

The Training Commission survey of employers' training activities defined 'on-the-job' as training:

1 which takes place at the *normal work position* of the trainee, not in a special training area or school;

2 where a manager or supervisor spends a *significant amount of time* with a trainee in order to teach a set of specific new skills that have been

3 *specified in advance;* and which includes periods of instruction where there may be *little or no useful output* in terms of products or service.

The definition was formulated in this way to ensure that the data collected related to on-the-job training with a clear learning element, rather than 'practice' while on the job.

Source: Sloman 1989

Figure 3.2   The Training Commission Definition of on-the-job Training

training and this affected its focus. From an HR viewpoint item 1, normal work position, can be taken to include normal briefing area used in team briefings. It should also include computer-based training (CBT). This training can be aimed very much at competences but the skills that are learned can be, and usually are, learned away from the specific work location and without immediate supervisor support (Sloman 1989). The important point in HR terms is that while training is a different sort of work it is still part of work. Everything should be geared to breaking down the barriers that separate work from training. Training is an everyday process.

Importance of on-the-job training

A major UK survey (Sloman 1989 and Training Commission 1988) has shown that a great deal of training takes place off-the-job. The

volume and costs of on- and off-the-job training in the UK are
shown in Figure 3.3.

In total in 1986–7 employers in Great Britain provided 125.4 million
days of training:

       64.7 million days off-the-job
       60.7 million days on-the-job

On average each employee received seven days' training a year:

       3.6 days off-the-job
       3.4 days on-the job

but more than half the employees received no training at all.

In total in 1986–7 employers in Great Britain spent £14.4 billion on
the provision of training for their workforce – just over £800 per
employee:

       £5.8 billion on off-the-job training
       £6.8 billion on on-the-job training
       £1.8 billion on training overheads

Source: Sloman 1989, reporting Training Commission 1988, a survey of
employers' training activities

Figure 3.3   Volume and Costs of Training

The extent of such training is encouraging but the HR manager
will be keen to ensure that this is good training which is adding to
the employee's competence. It must be *specifically directed*, with
feedback and *assessment* as essential ingredients. It is also important
to ensure that the standard of competence being sought is of the
level required and that the learning does not reinforce the *existing
bad habits* of trainers and supervisors. An awareness of these potential problems will ensure that on-the-job training is professionally
delivered. Figure 3.4 sets out some key principles against which the
success of on-the-job training, and indeed training generally, can
be measured.

Training must be specifically directed to a purpose.
Feedback on the effectiveness of training must follow.
Assessment off or on the job ensures standards.
Reinforce good not bad working practices.
Criteria for success should be set and monitored.

Figure 3.4   Principles of Training Success

Open learning

Some companies have long recognized the need for more structured learning among their employees. It is not sufficient to offer training within the limiting vision of what the company sees as important (necessary though that is). There must also be opportunities for employees to take the initiative to learn. This might cover learning that the company itself would not identify for a particular individual. Jaguar Cars is one example of a company that has established an open learning programme which complements the more specifically directed company learning programme. Giving employees freedom of access in this way also has an important effect on commitment-building and this is discussed further in Chapter 11.

Integrated training plans

The planning of human resources means that the planning of an integrated approach to training naturally follows. On-the-job and off-the-job training must be treated as complementary not alternative approaches. While there will always be questions of balance, both have their place. In terms of developing competence it is important that there is proper planning to answer the questions shown in Figure 3.5.

What is the training need?
How will it change?
How can training be delivered?
How should training be delivered on and off the job?
What financial support is available?
To what extent is a modular approach appropriate?
What use can be made of computer-based training?
How will competences be assessed?
Who will do the training?
Who 'owns' the training programme?
What are the company's plans for recruitment, retention and promotion?

Figure 3.5   Developing Integrated Training Plans

Value-added training

Many companies moving towards an HR environment are putting pressure on their HR director to demonstrate the value that training is adding to the organization. Awkward questions are being asked, for example about the effectiveness of internal training departments. Have they become stale and lost direction? What benefits might be obtained from radical approaches such as outsourcing, or passing operational responsibility to line managers, or using line managers as trainers?

The key to assessing added value is to have a business plan for training. Undertaking such an exercise must not be confused with a training needs analysis which comes much later. It is essential to understand the context in which the company or organization operates and therefore the business and financial opportunities that training must respond to.

Due to the speed of organizational change, learning objectives must become more specific. It has to be recognized that individuals have less time to learn than once was the case. With the increased cost of people's time, new ways have to be found to reduce costs and maximize the added value. For education and training to be set in a strategic framework, it is vital that the key essentials for learning are established. These 'learning drivers' as they are called include:

- needs-assessed skills or knowledge
- transition-focused training
- training activities
- competency-based skill development
- Business Issue Programmes.
  (From NM Johnston Orbis as Altas Corporation)

Once a company has established learning drivers, the delivery through new approaches can be explored. As the technology of training becomes more affordable and more available, it allows a variety of cost-effective delivery methods to be adopted. In the UK, Unipart have recently founded their own 'university' a move already common in the USA. There is a recognition of the need for widely available training and education that constantly updates and re-equips employees to enable them to meet tomorrow's problems.

The changing role of the trainer

The answers to the questions in Figure 3.5 lie at the heart of an integrated approach to human resource training. In summary, training is important and it should have a greater priority than many managers give it. Of course, that implies training staff emerging from what for many is relative isolation within the company or within the personnel department. If education and training belong at the forefront of planning for human resources then trainers must not let themselves be shunted to a siding. This implies a changed role and attitude by some trainers.

This centre-stage role will be new for many trainers, who may have been used to being the poor relations to their colleagues in industrial relations or reward management. The emphasis on competence-directed training changes the role of professional trainers. The inevitable consequence of rapid and technological change is that trainers will themselves have a problem of knowledge obsolescence. This is exacerbated by the emphasis on competence and skills training, at the expense of knowledge-directed training.

Another factor that affects this tendency has already been referred to – competence puts a premium on learning rather than teaching; and again the role of the trainer has to undergo a significant change.

The picture which will emerge therefore is of a powerful but small team of professional HR training facilitators. Their primary task will be to lead and motivate the drive for training rather than to undertake the training themselves. The actual conduct of a training session will just as likely be undertaken by supervisors and more senior managers as by professional trainers. Some of these supervisors may train for short sessions or may manage an overall programme. In the short term they would simply leave their job for a few hours, perhaps a day at the most. However, following practical experience and assessment, the most successful communicators and learning facilitators could be attached to the training section of the HR department for an extended period.

This flexible approach has a number of advantages for HR training:

1 The core training staff can be kept to a minimum, thus reducing costs.
2 Using managers after appropriate assessment ensures that training standards are maintained.
3 Using managers ensures that competence learning is based on the latest techniques and skills used in the workplace.
4 Training overheads will be considerably reduced.
5 Because of the attachments, line functions will retain greater 'ownership' of the training of their people.

To those advantages can be added the ability to respond and adapt to situations as they occur. It will be possible, with careful HR planning, to develop a stock of potential trainers which can be increased and reduced at short notice in response to demand. It also means that seasonality can be taken into account. For example, many organizations have periods when business is naturally slacker and it will be possible to draw on the managers as trainers during the slack period and allow them to return to their normal posts during the busy seasonal period. The principle of adapting training to utilize slow business periods applies equally, of course, to the employees themselves, who can be taken from their jobs when it suits the business activity. This practice has been adopted by many companies, but there is still greater room for change. In addition, the pressure to use such approaches will increase as the level of training increases to meet the organization's human resourcing needs.

The effect of such changes on professional trainers is that they become leader-facilitators rather than 'class teachers' in the traditional sense. Their role will be to stimulate support for education and training within the company. They will also have the crucial role of assessing, selecting (and of course training) the managers who will be acting as course tutors in a competence-based framework. The trainers will be responsible for programme design and the strategic planning of HR training as well as ensuring that the latest education and training techniques are absorbed into the organization's HR planning framework. Their expertise will be to understand how to make learning happen and to pass that skill on to the designated trainers.

Summary

Education and training (particularly taken together with employee development) are at the centre of planning for human resources. In the past far too little importance has been attached to training and the change in emphasis is one of the main requirements of a successful HR planning programme. At the same time, organizations in industry must develop close relationships with the state school and college service to ensure that their objectives complement and do not compete with one another. The role of professional trainers as leader-facilitators supported by managers as deliverers of training is crucial to enable up-to-date experience to be passed on and for line-function 'ownership' of training to be assured. Finally the importance of 'doing' rather than 'knowing' and of 'learning' rather than 'teaching', and the emphasis on competence-based training, is central to the planning of effective human resources.

Chapter 4

Benchmarking and Organizational Design

For the personnel function, discussion of organizational relationships has frequently conjured up the boring prospect of endless debate over structures. This is because the personnel function did not have a clear idea of what should be said about structures and, where it had, did not have a rigorous and consistent framework through which to develop a contribution.

HR provides both the need and the opportunity to reassess that situation. The need is provided because of the importance placed on people. An HR-based organization will want its people to develop and grow, and this cannot happen in a framework of constriction and resistance to change. In addition, the need for efficiency, adaptability and responsiveness to change ensures that a high priority is given to a flexible organization. The HR organization like any other is concerned with costs and it is not sensible to allow expensive waste to continue rather than face the issues involved. Finally, the maintenance of a well-designed organization or the retrieval of a bad one will not occur by accident. The organization will therefore rightly look to the planning of such matters in order to achieve success.

Hierarchies v cells

The traditional organization is seen as one that is based on a formal hierarchy exemplified and described in the 'family tree'. The classic structure represents the 'ideal' organization as shown in Figure 4.1. One person is at the top, three report to him or her, and three or four report to each of them. Eventually, at the routine operator level, a person can have 1–15 reporting to them. There is very quickly an urgent need for a large triangular piece of paper!

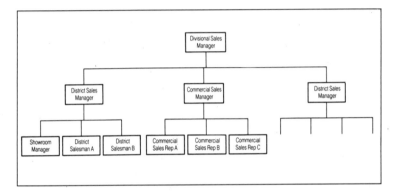

Figure 4.1   Classic Structure of an 'Ideal' Organization

The general assumption is that each level supervises the work of the lower level. Instructions are passed down and queries passed up.

The system is not without its advantages. Discipline is effective and decisions are carried out. There is limited room for interpretation because of the close control exercised. This means that a decision taken at the top can quickly be put into effect at some much lower level. There are organizations where this bureaucratic approach may be suitable, particularly where large numbers of people are involved in routine and repetitive tasks. The level of discipline is such that an order to behave in a certain way at a specified time is carried out. That is why the model remains necessary in much of the armed forces – if you want to order the advance of 100,000 men and their machines at the same time, you want very little room for creative interpretation. Imagine the results if each army, corps, divisional, brigade, battalion, company and platoon commander did his or her own creative thing!

Of course, the modern organization is dealing with change and variety – with a customer who expresses service in his or her own unique terms. In this environment many organizations have found the rigid hierarchy unsuitable for their needs.

The problem with the hierarchical approach is that when the job grows, the organization expands functions instead of cells. By cells I mean self-managing, self-contained units. A company with one engineer in charge of construction might expand. The cell approach would be to grow another cell – another construction manager. The hierarchical approach is to expand functions. Gradually you have separate design, drawing, site, architectural, project development and other functions. The result is that no one is in charge of the job and change is either impossible or random and expensive.

The HR approach to managing people requires that full use is made of personal development opportunities and a belief that success comes from creativity, not control. It is inevitable, therefore, that in looking at the future design of organizations, the HR planner will wish to question the extent to which a rigid hierarchical, functionally based structure has developed and whether it meets the organization's needs in coping with change.

The hierarchical approach brings with it another serious problem – the plethora of levels of reporting relationships.

The problem of too many managers

A study of UK organizations showed that many have structures which overlap. For many years personnel and productivity departments concentrated on improving efficiency on the 'shop floor'. By comparison, relatively little attention has been given to managers and improving their efficiency (Rowbottom and Billis 1987).

The managerial problem has arisen partly because of technological change. As work had a greater technological bias and routine work was handled by computers, it was inevitable that people would move into the offices in order to run and control those more complex systems. Most organizations, particularly those of any size, will have experienced either a growth in the numbers of employees classified as 'staff' or a relative change in the proportion of 'manual' to 'staff' employees in favour of the latter – usually office based.

Differentiation and the creation of levels

It was perhaps inevitable that the rapid growth which many organizations experienced has been relatively uncontrolled. As each new idea or need arose it was met by the creation of a new department or managerial team. This growth was also marked by another important but damaging phenomenon, differentiation. This is the managerial version of the shop-floor restrictive practice. The jobs managers held had different titles and (according to the self-imposed rules) required different qualifications. The result was that managers were not interchangeable and efficiency declined.

Differentiation had a second impact. As managers sought careers in ever narrower streams, they worked to ensure that there would be a suitable promotion structure. Organizations therefore created various and numerous levels of managers in order to satisfy their desire for progression. A plethora of 'assistants' and 'deputies' always gives the game away (see, for example, Figure 4.6(a) on page 54 below). What can they all be doing? The answer is probably – each others' jobs! There are simply more levels of managers than there are levels of work to be done.

Growth of levels as a response to failure

Technology and differentiation were not the only reason for the creation of extra levels. Figures 4.2(a) and (b) provide an example of another common cause. Figure 4.2(a) shows the organization of a sales team. It became apparent that the team as a whole was not selling the goods and following a review it was decided to 'strengthen' it. This led to the structure shown in 4.2(b).

The organization has now created itself some new problems. First, there will be an unclear relationship between the Field Sales Manager and the newly appointed Sales Executive. They will probably start competing for job territory. Secondly, whether or not they compete, there will be wasteful duplication. Because there are not two discrete levels of work, they will inevitably be doing each other's work. (This so called 'one-over-one' structure is almost invariably faulty.) Thirdly, the organization will have slowed down. There is now another level to go through, another meeting to have before a decision is taken, another person to persuade before

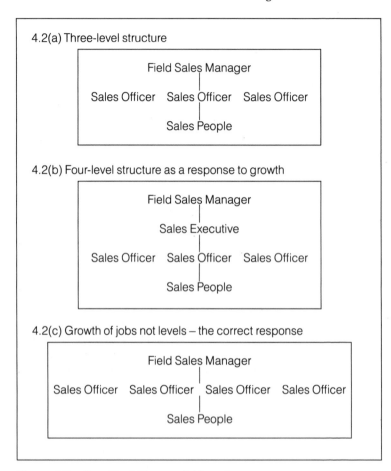

4.2(a) Three-level structure

Field Sales Manager

Sales Officer   Sales Officer   Sales Officer

Sales People

4.2(b) Four-level structure as a response to growth

Field Sales Manager

Sales Executive

Sales Officer   Sales Officer   Sales Officer

Sales People

4.2(c) Growth of jobs not levels – the correct response

Field Sales Manager

Sales Officer   Sales Officer   Sales Officer   Sales Officer

Sales People

Figure 4.2   Growth of Managerial Levels

anything is changed.

The solution to this problem, however, is fairly obvious. It is more jobs, not more levels, which are needed. The result is shown in Figure 4.2(c).

Stifling creativity and other costs

This inefficiency is bad enough simply because of the cost involved. More people have to be serviced within the organization; wages have to be paid, holidays controlled and covered for and office space provided. However, from an HR viewpoint, the direct cost consideration, while important, is only part of the problem. As already discussed, a key feature of the HR-based organization is the importance placed on people as the key to growth and creativity. The problem of the multi-layered bureaucratic organizational structure is the damaging effect it has on creativity and growth. Because there is someone else to refer a decision to, there is another barrier to change, and the result is either a slowing down of change or sterility such that change is not even attempted.

The struggle for territory and office politics

One further reason for this restriction on growth and creativity is that when managers' jobs overlap they are constantly fighting territorial battles to preserve their own patch. This often exhibits itself in terms of 'office politics'. The naïve consider that the destruction caused by politics can be resolved by team building. Such efforts are wasted unless the conditions that led to the destructive behaviour are removed. This requires a clear delineation of each manager's role, distinguishing it from that of another manager. (A second requirement is a clear statement of goals and objectives and this is discussed in Chapter 6.)

An HR response

How are these problems to be faced? It may be helpful to refer again to Figure 4.2(a) and (b). The poor sales might have arisen from a number of causes. The Field Sales Manager might not have been up to the job and might not have been giving proper leadership. It could have been that the sales officers were not up to their jobs and needed retraining and personal development. Or perhaps there was simply too much work to do and each sales officer (or the Field Sales Manager) was trying to cover too large a territory.

Of course in the example in Figure 4.2(b) these problems were not faced and the symptoms only were being tackled. As things were going off the rails the solution was simple – 'Bring in some control and get a grip on the situation.' In Figure 4.2(b) the organization has failed to solve the original problem and in creating an extra level of manager has added a few more.

Before leaving this example, I should sound a note of caution to ensure that this point is not treated too lightly. Problems of the type looked at above are often not faced, perhaps for the very good reason that the solution may be extremely painful. In 4.2(a), suppose that the sales problem arose because the sales officers could not cope with the job. Perhaps technological change has meant that their company has moved into new fields. The example was drawn from a company which had moved with technology from typewriters and adding machines to personal computers (PCs). The perceived result was that sales officers were out of their depth. A planned HRD strategy might have ensured that the employees kept pace with the changes, although rapid technological developments could make that difficult. If the conclusion is that the organization has too many of the wrong sort of people, it is hardly surprising (though wrong) that the painful conclusion was avoided. An HR strategy can lead to a more effective organization but the difficulties of implementation may require immense effort.

Identifying organizational levels

In order to avoid having too many levels, or removing them when they exist, some method of determining organizational levels is required. There is no single solution and those that exist are based heavily on common sense, such as avoiding putting advisers into a line relationship and so on.

One method of identifying work levels which shows some promise was described by Rowbottom and Billis (1987). The research, based on work at Brunel University, draws examples from many types of organization – government, health services, banking, insurance and manufacturing. The core of the approach is a belief that there are five possible work levels in any organization. These are shown in Figure 4.3.

The authors recognize that in the largest organizations there may be a sixth or even a seventh level. This does not however affect the basic proposition that each work level requires one level of operator. Managerial work requires few levels.

It is this concentration of responsibility in one person at any

1 Prescribed output
This level of work involves concrete tasks whose end-products are completely prescribed or prescribable (eg typing a letter from manuscript, checking an invoice, making a component to a set specification, carrying out a standard reception procedure).

2 Situational response
These are again concrete tasks, but at this level the appropriate end-product can no longer be prescribed before the event (eg composing a letter, producing a rounded report, appraising a subordinate, assessing the essential needs of a customer or client).

3 Systematic provision
This level of work goes beyond dealing one by one with concrete cases (however complex) to meeting a whole flow of them (eg developing a better procedure for handling orders or complaints, installing and running a new production or data-processing system).

4 Comprehensive provision
Work at this level is not just developing or running one system of service or production but providing a comprehensive range to meet the needs of some whole market, territorial society or organization, with all the associated strategic planning, budgeting, and capital development that follows. Examples are running a large manufacturing facility or developing and maintaining the complex nursing organization for the whole of a large general hospital. Staff concerned are often called 'directors' or 'general managers' (although titles alone are never definitive of level).

5 Field coverage
Here the activity is not just providing some given range of services or facilities but considering the whole of the field of action concerned (scientific instruments, leisure services, health services or whatever) to settle just what kinds of things to pursue and within what general parameters. The job of chief executive of a £15–150 million turnover enterprise is probably pitched at this level, but note again the title 'chief executive' is used at various other levels as well, sometimes down to level 3.

Source: Rowbottom and Billis 1987

Figure 4.3   Organizational Levels of Work

particular level that gives the structure its strength. In respect of Figure 4.2, if it was assessed that there was more work than three sales officers could cope with, the correct approach would be to create a fourth sales officer, not a sales executive and therefore an extra level. This theme is demonstrated in the Brunel work referred to above. If we analyse the work being done in the organizations described in Figure 4.4, the following is found:

		Number of levels in practice	*Actual levels of work*
(a)	Large factory	6	4
(b)	Large welfare agency	9	5

The extra levels of managers/operators do not truly reflect the levels of work which have to be done. Inevitably costs increase and confusion abounds. There will be ample opportunities for duplication, frustration and the destruction of creative effort. A solution to the problem is shown in Figure 4.4. Here the organization has been divided into the actual levels of work. By removing levels from the organization it will be possible to achieve reduced costs and a streamlined operation. Again, however, the difficulty of achieving the changes demanded by this HR approach should not be underestimated.

There are two ways of removing the levels; by taking them out of a 'line' relationship, and by removing the posts altogether. If attempts are made to remove the posts altogether, there will be difficulties if the surplus employees have nowhere to go and redundancy is necessary. In an expanding organization or one where the age of managers makes retirement a possibility, these problems can be handled. This may not be so easy where the identification of a surplus threatens employees with redundancy they do not want.

The alternative of taking people out of a line relationship is not simple either. There may be a perceived loss of status if someone is moved to an advisory role, and this may well be resisted. This will particularly be the case where 'being where the action is' is seen as a prerequisite for personal satisfaction and subsequent promotion.

A second approach to identifying organizational levels is to use a job evaluation technique. The use of job evaluation for determining pay brings its own problems to an HR environment and this is

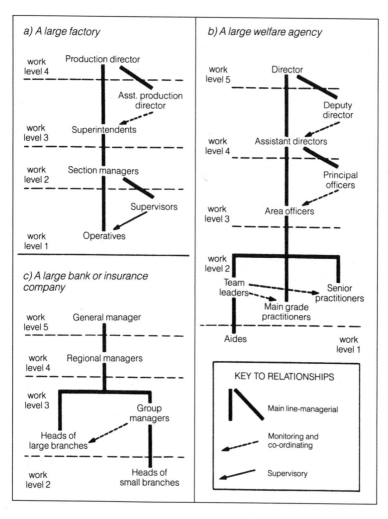

Source: Rowbottom and Billis 1987

Figure 4.4   Organization Charts showing Expected Work Levels

discussed in Chapter 7. But the underlying theory can be exploited to analyse organizational levels.

Span of control

As will be seen in Chapter 7, job evaluation is about determining the relative 'size' and 'weight' of jobs within an organization. The Hay method establishes a scale of measurement as a way of deciding the size of gaps between jobs. The measurement scale is applied to what are seen as key components of jobs:

- know-how (the knowledge and experience required to perform the job),
- problem-solving (the degree of 'self-starting' thinking required in the job),
- accountability (the extent to which the occupant is responsible for action and for the consequences of that action)

The judgements are based on rigorously tested systematic criteria, and the whole job is assigned 'job units'. These might vary as follows in a typical organization:

	Units
Managing Director	2128
Sales Director	1372
Regional Sales Manager	955
Area Sales Manager	682
Sales Representative	301

In this way, so-called 'steps' are identified and each is assessed as being around 15 per cent in terms of job units. In general terms an analysis of these differences between jobs shows that at one step differences are just discernible, at two steps differences are reasonably clear, and at three steps differences are immediately evident.

It is not necessary to discuss the detail here but the analysis is able to demonstrate that three steps' difference between levels of job removes the worst problems of overlap and ensures that jobs at these different levels are not competing with each other for the same work. Of course it would be possible to apply the three-step rule mechanically in determining operational levels throughout the organization but that will be seen as unnecessarily rigid by many users (although some European, particularly West German, companies appear to prefer the certainty provided by such an approach).

In practice, some flexibility can be allowed and differences of two and four steps are possible. The important point is that the step analysis highlights potential problem areas. If the step differences are close, there are probably too many levels of management in the organization. If the step differences are too great, then people will be trying to bridge gaps in responsibility that are beyond their knowledge, experience and perhaps their general level of ability.

In practical use such approaches have been found to be self-checking and internally consistent. There are difficulties in application (such as preparing an analysis of organizational work and writing detailed job descriptions in a consistent and specific manner) but the result can provide valuable insights into where levels of management are overprovided.

Dispensing with myths

In any analysis of organizational design the HR planner will face a number of difficulties. The urge for promotion and status may well result in pressure for new false high-level jobs to be created, resulting in a profusion of deputies, assistants, seniors and the like. The difficulties of coping with status and job losses have been referred to above, but there are other key HR considerations. The six principles are set out in Figure 4.5.

Spans of control can vary and be significant. Depending on the job it is possible to supervise two or 30 people successfully. However, the type of work will be an important factor. It is easier to supervise 30 people doing similar routine tasks than five people doing disparate tasks.

People can be paid *different* salaries at the *same* organizational level. It is important that the organization is not stifled, for example in employee development, because the people needing development are at the wrong hierarchical level.

Similar jobs can be *paid differently*. There is no reason why all jobs at a level have to be the same or receive the same salary. That is the thinking that leads to lengthy decision-making processes as every person on a different grade insists on being involved.

People on higher salaries do not have to be 'in charge' of *everyone*

1	Spans of control can vary and be significant.
2	Different salaries can be paid at the same level.
3	Similar jobs can be paid differently.
4	People do not have to be in charge of all those below them.
5	There should be significant responsibility gaps between jobs.
6	There should be room for rewarding performance and a facility for development.

Figure 4.5   The Six Principles of Organizational Design in Human Resourcing

on a lower salary. This is an extension of the previous point: an organization can be streamlined by *widening* spans of control and making them *less* deep (see Figures 4.6(a) and (b) for a good and fairly typical example).

There should be significant responsibility gaps between jobs, since without this jobs are bound to overlap and increase conflict between managers. And finally, there should be room for *rewarding performance* and *providing for development*. This can be 'designed' into the organization but only if a flexible approach is adopted.

These points go against the established practice within many personnel departments. It is only through the removal of the old myths that organizations can be streamlined. The difference in efficiency would be significant.

There is one further myth that can be dispelled. There is a fear that an organization with fewer levels provides fewer promotion opportunities and that this will result in staff becoming disenchanted. But this need not be the case. A steep multi-level structure may provide the opportunity for promotion but it also provides a stultifying 'non-self-actualizing' experience. The HR organization operating the principles in Figure 4.5 can provide promotion by rewarding managers while at the same level; it is not necessary to justify every reward by a change in job title and a move up a level of management, however marginal the difference. Moreover, at any level the people above and below are doing clearly different jobs, so there are more opportunities for creative development of the job. In this way, the HR organization hopes to achieve the personal fulfilment that is necessary without resorting to the artificial creation of unnecessary levels or other disfunctional status plays.

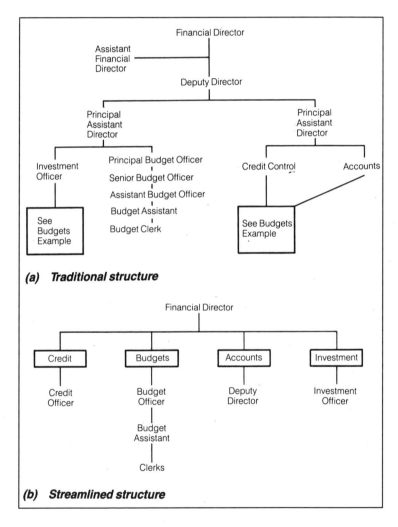

Figure 4.6   Streamlining Organizational Structures

Benchmarking

Of course, all this analysis of organization design is of limited value
if there are arguments about how big the organization should be for
a given amount of work. One technique that shows considerable
promise is that of benchmarking (Fitz-enz 1993). Benchmarking is
the continuous search for best practices (and the people needed to
do them) which can be adapted to lead an organization to improved
performance. The search for best or better practice entails finding
departments or businesses/organizations that meet your department specification and then closely analysing what they do and
whether they achieve superior performance in either costs or quality terms.

Of course 'best' practice is subjective and transitory, and this
neatly fits into the fluid framework of HR with its emphasis on
customers and quality. The search for a quality product that meets
customers' needs is a perpetual journey not a destination. Even
while a quality product is being delivered successfully to approving
customers, an HR quality organization is looking to the next
improvement, the next change.

Choosing partners in benchmarking

Benchmarking also assumes a commonality of background conditions. There is no purpose in trying to compare the people and
processes used if the comparator tasks are quite differently handled
and do not meet the defined requirements of your own organization. This latter point is important. A comparison may show that a
process is handled by many fewer people and in a way not considered satisfactory by the host organization. It is important that the
comparison is not rejected out of hand – it may be the key to a
significant breakthrough in cost reduction and quality improvement.

The choice of partners for comparison is therefore very important
and is affected by such factors as availability and size. In a multi-
division company it may be possible to find suitable *internal comparators* carrying out tasks that are sufficiently similar to one's own.
Starting at home is, anyway, essential for a clear understanding of
processes. In any event, internal benchmarking is probably necessary in order to have information that is subsequently of use to an

outside organization. It is unlikely that an organization will join in a benchmarking exercise if the giving process is all one way.

The second type of partner that can be chosen is a *competitor*. The problems here are that, while practices may well be comparable and therefore provide data of probable direct relevance, there are problems created by commercial confidentiality. The closer the information you require is to the core of what they perceive as competitive advantage, the greater will be the reluctance to share the information.

Finally it is possible to refer to *industry* analysis where people are engaged in similar activities but are not in direct competition. Here the practices are likely to be similar and therefore the data will be more generally applicable. Data will also be easily shared. Of course, against that must be set the difficulty of size and geographic differences and possibly cultural problems, especially where international boundaries are crossed. The different partners and their respective advantages and disadvantages are set out in Figure 4.7.

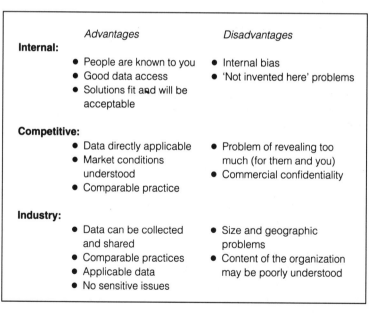

Source: Fitz-enz 1993 (adapted)

Figure 4.7   Advantages and Disadvantages of Partners

Understanding performance drivers

Performance drivers are the crucial group of factors that determine what makes an organization tick. They will include the growth rate and technology the company is engaged in. For example, if you are a stable long-term organization dealing in long lead times (say, electricity generation), the performance drivers will be quite different from those that apply to newspaper or periodical publishers. Performance drivers also embrace the cultural conditions in which you operate. This is particularly important, as culture may get in the way of change and a clear understanding of culture will tell you how appropriate any suggested practices are to your organization. It is sensible to analyse the performance drivers that apply to your organization in a manner such as that set out in Figure 4.8.

Internal					
Culture	1	2	3	4	5
	Low Key				High Key
Size	1		2		3
	< 100		250–500		1000 +
Resources	1		2		3
	People Intensive				Capital Intensive
External					
Information	1		2		3
	Available				Not Available
Regulations	1		2		3
	Low				Highly Regulated
Technology	1		2		3
	Low/Stable				High/Charging

Figure 4.8   Performance Drivers

Of course, these are only examples but they should illustrate the point of the exercise, which is to match yourself as closely as possible with a comparator. The organizations being compared must have something in common, for if you try and benchmark where there is no similarity the exercise is certain to fail (Fitz-enz 1990).

Summary and conclusion

The main argument in this chapter is that, for people's creativity to be released, it is essential to ensure that employees are not prevented from taking decisions at their level of work. And where items have to be referred for a decision, it is important to facilitate the process of decision-making by having as few levels as possible to refer to. In addition to the barriers to creativity and progress caused by having surplus operating/managerial levels, the costs involved can be high. These problems can be addressed either by designing new organizations or, alternatively, by assessing the effectiveness of existing ones. This is a process in which benchmarking has proved to be particularly beneficial.

Finally, there is a need to challenge many established beliefs about status and to apply the six principles of organizational design in an HR environment.

Chapter 5
Flexibility and the Flexible Firm

One of the key objectives of a human resourcing approach to managing people is the achievement of flexibility in the workforce. The concept of flexible organizations is certainly not new. Manpower planners have always recognized the limitations of an approach that sought the 'right' forecast.

> In preparing 'plans' the need for flexibility is stressed. No plan in any fixed sense will be relevant for long. The success of planning in an organization will be judged by how well the organization can anticipate or adapt to the unforeseen. (Bramham 1975)

Human resources planning has drawn on, extended and codified those concepts of flexibility into a body of knowledge popularized as the 'flexible firm'. The HR perspective has changed much of the original thinking about flexibility which was seen in structural rather than human terms. The 1980s literature spoke of 'numerical', 'functional' and 'financial' flexibility (reported in Atkinson 1985). These terms (apart from being shrouded in the academic's preference for using new jargon to describe everyday ideas) suffered from a failure to recognize the human dimension. The human resource viewpoint is that flexibility is first an attitude of mind and therefore commitment and teamwork are essential prerequisites for the 'flexible firm'. The problem for the researcher is that commitment is not easy to study and even less easy to measure. This in part explains the desire to see *structural* change as concrete evidence of flexibility (IS 1986).

Terms of flexibility

It is possible to identify at least eight forms of flexibility in the organization as shown in Figure 5.1.

TRAINING	– SKILLS FLEXIBILITY
OCCUPATION	– JOB FLEXIBILITY
MOBILITY	– LOCATION FLEXIBILITY
WORKING TIME	– WORK PATTERN FLEXIBILITY
ORGANIZATION	– DEPARTMENT FLEXIBILITY
NUMERICAL	– NUMBERS FLEXIBILITY
FINANCIAL	– WAGE COST FLEXIBILITY
ATTITUDE	– EMPLOYEES' VIEW OF FLEXIBILITY

Figure 5.1   Types of Flexibility

Skills flexibility

Skills flexibility deals with the essential areas of training and education. In HR terms the emphasis is on *skills* rather than *knowledge*. This reflects the importance to the company of what an employee can *do* rather than what she or he *knows*. This emphasis reflects the modern concept of competence-based training and the rejection of time-serving as a satisfactory approach. It is also important to recognize that in planning for flexible human resources it is not simply a matter of providing more training, although more training may well take place. The point of flexibility is to build an environment and to encourage attitudes such that employees do what has to be done without reference to irrelevant demarcations. In the UK at least, such demarcations based on skill barriers have proved a menace to organizational improvement.

In 1984 and 1985 Income Data Services (IDS) prepared special reports on flexibility (Income Data Services 1985). The reports commented that while on paper the barriers were being removed the practice did not reflect the theory. On the other hand, the new technologies in, for example, the printing industry have forced through significant changes in skills barriers. Indeed there is some evidence that technology and economic forces are key determinants in achieving flexibility. Unless the 'writing is on the wall' there can be little to motivate either managers or employees to accept the (particularly short-term) pain that follows from fundamental changes in attitudes to skill demarcations.

Of course skills flexibility cannot be achieved without a thorough review and overhaul of training within the company. The search is for a modular approach to training whereby employees can gather skills at different times. It is also important that basic training is generalized across as many skill areas as possible. The training of young people in the UK is particularly important in this respect. The training is either too long and academic (particularly craft areas) or virtually non-existent (semi- and unskilled jobs). It is already known that training in shorter, more intensive bursts, and more generically oriented, is both possible and fruitful.

It is important for the successful planning of human resources that the old attitudes are challenged and new methods adopted. It goes without saying that this flexibility should be directed towards age and sex, two common forms of discrimination. With employment pressure increasing for many organizations it makes little sense to restrict entrants to many jobs to those (usually males!) aged around 16–17.

Job flexibility

Provision must also be made for upgrading the skills of the semi- and unskilled categories. Trade unions often argue that organizations do not make sufficient use of the people they employ. With new approaches to training, many people could be given access to jobs from which they are currently barred. It should also be recognized, of course, that training is not the only problem, although anyone who has been involved in trying to make changes in the UK City and Guilds courses and the education service will perhaps regard this as enough of a barrier to contend with. The greater problem is in fact the attitudinal problem of people. Demarcation springs from a desire to protect one's job and personal continuity by restricting access to the role, restricting what the role includes and restricting the transfer of duties to other roles. In the UK this type of occupational inflexibility is usually associated with manual workers. (Please note how the words 'manual' and 'worker', as opposed to 'staff' and 'employee', naturally go together.) This itself is a reflection of the UK distaste for 'trade'. The separation between 'worker' and 'employee' subtly suggests that staff do not actually 'work'; they are engaged in an altogether much finer activity! (The manual worker, meanwhile, is seen as nothing more than an extension of the machine-tool in the production process.)

The inflexibility among occupations is wasteful and expensive. It mitigates against change and prevents the company adapting to new circumstances. Many managers have struggled for years against trade union opposition and management indifference to this problem. The failure to develop flexible occupations and therefore reduce costs and improve efficiency was a key factor in the death of many UK companies and industries such as shipbuilding, motorcycle and car manufacture, watch-making, television manufacture and so on. Not that change has not been achieved. Ford UK may have failed by its own standards but the number of job categories there have reduced from 516 in 1986 to about 45 in 1988.

Flexible attitudes should, of course, go far beyond flexibility among manual job categories. The same principles extend to clerks, telephonists, typists, salesmen and the plethora of engineering titles. Finally, flexibility might usefully be extended into those traditional middle-class preserves of medicine, teaching, the law and accountancy. It is somewhat ironic to listen to the self-justification of the professions as to why they should escape the flexibility that they so eagerly sought to apply to their lesser brethren! Of course all professional middle-class restrictive practices apparently operate in the public interest (as with the response to the Mackay proposals on the English legal profession).

Mobility

In order to achieve flexibility the organization will usually have to improve mobility. This would not include moving from job to job – that would properly be regarded as occupational flexibility. Mobility means removing the barriers to the physical relocation of the employee. It can be of at least two types. At one level a long-distance geographical move is involved, which will involve relocating the employee's home. The company can greatly assist in this process by the variety of schemes available for house loans, differential house cost assistance, settling in allowances and so on. This type of mobility is important, particularly at the managerial level. Cost and human resistance often preclude geographical mobility at lower levels in the hierarchy. However, the management can assist by improving infrastructure and developing a freer housing market.

On a local level mobility is also important and perhaps more so because resistance is more widespread. Mobility has to be achieved between buildings, different work sites and departments. Along with this desire to move people there must be a recognition of the importance of teams in ensuring good team-work. Mobility must, therefore, be seen as an enriching experience and not a burden to be endured.

Working time

The traditional trade union approach to working time has been to concentrate working hours in as few days as possible (usually five days in a week) and as few hours in the day (9–5 for office workers and 8–4 for manual employees). There has always been flexibility through systems but that was motivated by the needs of the production process rather than through a desire for flexibility itself.

The concentration on customers' needs and employees' desires has brought new pressures on working time. Changing social patterns mean that many customers expect a service that does not fit with traditional work patterns. The need to provide flexible working arrangements to meet this need is particularly noticeable in the retail and service sectors.

The type of flexibility needed would be to allow the organization to operate on more days of the week and for longer periods on any particular day. A typical retail example would be to operate on seven days a week from 8am to 10pm but with employees still working four, five or six days and around 35–40 hours per week.

This type of flexibility also allows the use of part-time employees who are thus able to fit their restricting personal arrangements into the patterns of organizational needs.

The difficulty of human resource planning in such an environment should not be underestimated. Absence, holidays and supervision will need very careful handling. Team building must also be considered because without special provision and attention separate workforces will effectively become established – perhaps offering different levels and types of service!

Organizational flexibility

If you ask UK managers how they earn a living, the response will be 'I am a chemical engineer', or 'I am an accountant'. If the same question is asked of a Japanese the response would be 'I work for Sony' (or whichever company). This neatly sums up the problem for many companies. The loyalty is to the occupation and not to the organization. It is no wonder that demarcations and restrictive practices were built up, continue and are defended with such vigour.

The functionally controlled hierarchy in many organizations serves to reinforce this inflexibility. The answer is to concentrate the first loyalty not on the function or occupation but on the organization. In this way supervisors, clerks, maintenance technicians etc will more easily accept the move to another department. As with other forms of flexibility, it is important that the legal contract and terms of recruitment establish flexibility as a basic philosophy of the organization.

Numerical and pay flexibility

One obvious way of resolving problems of forecasting human resources is to make the process less important. All the above approaches to flexibility are directed to increasing organizational adaptability. Numerical and financial flexibility is aimed at creating flexibility in recruitment and retention by the balancing of part-time and full-time employees and overtime. Bonus and incentive schemes can also affect the output of employees and are therefore a useful factor in numerical control.

A key method is to reduce lead times for training where this can be done consistently with maintaining quality. This allows recruitment to be done nearer to actual need and reduces the risk and extent of shortages and surpluses.

Financial flexibility is concerned with the payment of employees. Pay structures can encourage or hinder flexibility within the company. High pay will tend to assist recruitment and increase retention while low pay will do the reverse. At the same time pay can be used in a specifically targeted way to achieve the recruitment and retention of particular problem categories. Of course such targeted payments can lead to resistance among other employees if perceptions of fairness are breeched and the reasons for the targeted supplements are not accepted.

Employee attitude

The attitude of employees to flexibility is crucial. (Incidentally it is also important to gain the commitment of contractors and suppliers but that should involve those employees in their commitment relationship with their own employers.) Any criticism of the flexibility discussions of the 1980s will probably concern the lack of attention to gaining the employees' commitment to that flexibility. Among those managers who believe in the 'technical' rather than the 'human' organization there is an expectation that improvement will follow any procedural change. In this analysis flexibility would be achieved by a company reorganization or a new agreement with trade unions. The IDS survey (Income Data Services 1985), and a multitude of failed company flexibility agreements, are sufficient evidence of the failure to implement the theory of flexibility in practice because of the lack of a positive and supportive attitude.

The question of employee attitude is central to human resourcing and is given greater attention in Chapter 11.

Employees and outworkers

This flexibility can apply to the company's workers (not 'employees' as they are not all employed) at three levels, as shown in Figure 5.2. In more detail these are:

- prime employees (direct employees on permanent contracts)
- secondary employees (who will be direct employees but on temporary or part-time contracts)
- outworkers (who will not be employees at all but contractors, agency staff, consultants and so on).

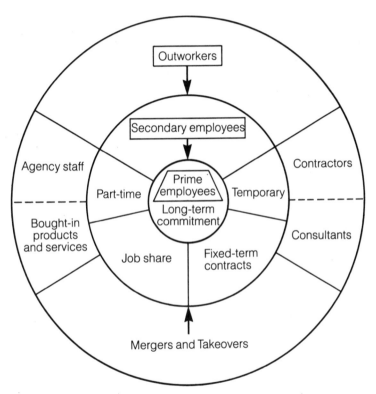

Figure 5.2   The Flexibility Map

The focus is on the supply of manpower. This concentration on supply is a recognition of the unlikelihood of ever being able to forecast future requirements in more than a rough and ready manner. In the face of inaccurate assessments of the future, and the need to adapt to any change that might occur, the solution is internal flexibility. This can involve flexibility among prime employees who can do a wide range of jobs over a variety of working hours, or the ability to bring in new secondary employees or outworkers on fixed-term contracts which are continued only when required. (Leek 1985; Atkinson 1985).

This type of flexibility is the strategic answer to the difficulties experienced by managers who have lost the ability to 'hire and fire' at will. Of course the demands on prime employees are likely to be high as they will undertake a variety of jobs at a variety of locations and learn new skills as required. It therefore follows that their personal commitment is crucial and this is why a prerequisite for flexibility is a flexible attitude on the part of the employee. This need for personal commitment in turn requires the organization to focus on the employee as an asset not as a liability or cost.

Trade unions and flexibility

Although the trade unions in the context of human resource planning are discussed in Chapter 9, it is worth highlighting possible problems in the flexible approach. It will be essential not to go beyond what is acceptable to employees in terms of flexibility. One approach is to pay premiums for unsocial hours. If the customer is willing to pay the extra cost and the employee is willing to work then presumably that is a satisfactory arrangement.

Trade unions have expressed strong reservations (Trade Union Research Unit 1984). The trade unions, and perhaps employees, see in flexibility an attack on hard-won terms and conditions. The mining unions fought for many years for an end to the six-day week only to find that in the 1990s, technology had made it necessary again.

At the same time flexibility could become a byword for insecurity and a casualized workforce. Of course this would not be human resource planning. An organization which behaved as though employees could be taken on or dispensed with at a moment's notice would hardly be seeking to achieve employee commitment as its first priority and as an essential step in building teams and developing quality products or services.

There is no reason why 'casual' employees cannot be integrated into the company in new ways. Many companies are finding that home or teleworkers need a different sort of social provision but it can be catered for. This has occurred with women who leave to have children. A properly managed skills retention scheme can make a virtue out of occasional employment both for the company and the employee. For example, an ex-employee on skills retention will be invited to social functions, updated about company changes and be able to work at short notice or occasionally to cover sickness or holidays and may subsequently return to 'prime' employment.

The position with regard to suppliers, contractors or agency employees is even more straightforward. Those companies have employees who will look to their company as their focus for commitment. There is no reason why such an employment package should be seen as undermining employees.

There is, perhaps, an area where trade unions will undergo an important change, at least in the UK. Human resource planning achieved in part through flexible working will weaken the traditional means by which trade unions and employees have sought to control organizations. With flexible working this sort of control is impossible. It is certainly a new situation for many trade unions and it is up to the organization to ensure that it is not seen by employees as a threat. Inevitably the moment of first change will not be easy as old shiboleths are threatened and then cast aside.

The Trades Union Congress (TUC) in the UK has, on balance, recognized that flexibility can be good for employees. The TUC appreciates that flexibility allows for better and wider provision of training, opens up new job opportunities and gives the hope of more satisfying jobs (TUC Annual Report 1988). With respect to the 'shop floor', perhaps the loss of power on a day-to-day basis will be a good thing – trade unions in Germany manage to stay in business by initiating ideas and not restricting them. If the UK trade union movement mirrored that practice perhaps managers would prefer it.

Summary

Flexibility is an important part of the process by which human resource planning can overcome problems of forecasting and adapting to the unforeseen. At the same time efficiency can be increased and costs reduced. For employees variety and opportunities for personal development will enrich jobs. At the same time flexible working provides an opportunity for employees who cannot work full hours. The eight aspects of flexibility are skills flexibility, job flexibility, location flexibility (mobility), time flexibility, department flexibility, numbers and wage flexibility and the flexibility of employees' attitudes, and all should be explored. There is also a need for trade unions to recognize the importance of flexibility and the removal of restrictions.

Chapter 6

Objectives, Performance and Productivity

The purpose of good objectives

One of the aims of human resource planning is to create a situation in which employees know what is going on in the organization and understand what their contribution is. The employee will in turn be committed to the success of the organization and the needs of the employee will be in harmony with those of the organization. Indeed a fundamental tenet of human resourcing is to focus on employees and their needs, believing that only in this way can true commitment, and all the benefits that flow from it, emerge and develop.

This is not as easy as it might sound. There are many organizations that have not made clear where they are or where they are going. Quite simply, objectives for the organization and the employee are not always set out and integrated in a workable manner. This may be due to stupidity and incompetence. It is more likely to be due to a failure to come to terms with the conflicts between managers, employees and other stakeholders (eg owners, shareholders, suppliers, trade unions, governments) about why the organization exists. This is a reflection of the failure to handle the power and political aspects which run through all behaviour and are discussed separately in Chapter 14. This failure to handle such conflicts leads to attempts to fudge the issues.

Stated policy and done policy

A rather neat way of illustrating this point and the problems that arise with objectives is used by E. Harker at British Telecom in Newcastle Upon Tyne. This is the concept of the 'stated' policy and the 'done' policy. Stated policies are those objectives and performance targets that the company says it is trying to achieve – company policy. Then there is the done policy, which is what *actually* happens within the organization.

There may be differences between stated and done policies as a result of a failure to achieve an objective, despite attempts to do so, but this is not the type of difference this representation is aiming at. What it aims to show is that in many organizations the difference is often cynical, and the company never intended to do what was stated.

Given that a key intention of human resource planning is to ensure that objectives are set, this concept can be effective in training and development for highlighting the problems involved. Figure 6.1 shows the result of one group's assessment of the stated and done policy in action. It was through this sort of identification that the clear differences and conflicts were resolved. This is important. When the cynical separation between stated and done policies is exposed, it can be tackled. Like the vampire, negative political behaviour finds it difficult to survive in the light!

STATED POLICY	DONE POLICY
Reduce costs	No budgeting control; wasted expenditure
Employees are an asset	Little attempt to train or develop employees
Teamwork is crucial	Employees treated divisively and with thinly disguised contempt
Priority on achieving market share increase	Sales force cut-back to reduce costs
Cost savings must be sought	Thousands spent on new executive suite of offices

Figure 6.1   A Typical Example of Stated and Done Policies

It is also necessary to separate off the sharply expressed and easily understood company policies expressed as generalized statements. They are of limited value in setting an employee's work objectives except perhaps as a general backcloth to provide perspective. These 'mission statements' are useful in terms of providing a focus for team building. They can also provide an identity for external consumption or for courses and conferences. They are not useful for the day-to-day management and control at the workplace, where specific criteria of achievement are required.

Done policy is, then, a recognition of what happens in many organizations. The stated policy is what the objectives are stated to be by the company but the done policy is what actually happens. This difference can be seen after a team briefing where the manager, having extolled the virtues of team building and working together then breaks for lunch. Luncheon tickets are handed out by the secretary while the manager winds his way to the waitress service restaurant! The stated policy was team-work; the done policy was 'I deserve somewhere better to eat than you.'

Try this for yourselves. Set out your stated policies and see if they match your done policies. Even better, try it with supervisors and team leaders – they are usually the focal point at which a company's discordant objectives meet.

Of course this difference between stated and done policy appears to start early in life. How many of us challenged our parents' behaviour only to be told 'Do as I say not do as I do!'? We do not have this luxury with responsible employees. An HR environment cannot permit double standards. Every effort must be made to integrate and dovetail policies at the individual and corporate level. Without this, there will be no commitment and teams and team-work will not develop.

The nature of good objectives

Talk about performance presupposes that the organization has some way of setting achievement criteria and then measuring what has been done.

There have been a variety of attempts in management thinking to come to terms with objectives and objective setting. Management by objectives (MBO) was one of the most successful and it went through various periods of enthusiasm and disillusionment. Whatever you call it, there can be no doubt that without objectives you cannot make much sense of assessing performance and ensuring that production targets and productivity levels have been achieved.

There are a number of important principles that must be followed and these are summarized in Figure 6.2. First, and perhaps most important, objectives against which achievement will be measured must be expressed in a *simple* and *clear* manner. They should preferably also be *measurable*. If they are not, problems of rewarding performance will arise. Therefore, generalized statements of the type 'care at all times for the customer' are of no value at the task, objective-setting, end of the business. In terms of absence it is not sensible to have an objective to 'improve attendance levels'. However a quantifiable target to 'reduce sickness absence from 8.4 per cent to 7.9 per cent by 1 January 1990' makes much more sense.

Objectives should be:

simply and clearly expressed

measurable

supported by the doer

tough but achievable

applied to all employees

few in number

integrated with other employees' objectives

Figure 6.2 Principles of Good Objectives

Secondly, objectives should be *supported* by the person who is to achieve them. If a work objective is imposed or even worse if the recipient does not understand it, it is not likely that much will be achieved.

Thirdly, objectives should be *tough* but *achievable*. Most people will find it difficult to respond to what they see as impossible dreaming on the part of the senior manager. Equally, however, a shrewd manager will be tempted to go for understating likely achievements when objectives are being set. It is rather like playing the budget game – the manager keeps a bit in reserve!

Fourthly, objectives should be applied to *all* employees. There should be no hierarchical cut-off. This is important if team-work is to be established and if we are to achieve the commitment of all employees to the enterprise.

Fifthly, there should not be *too many* objectives. If you are working on 20 priorities everyone knows the truth – that you have *no* priorities – and employees will act accordingly. Objectives must be few enough in number to handle at any one time.

Finally, they should be *integrated*. This means linking personal objectives with those of the department or company and in turn ensuring consistency with the objectives of other managers and employers.

The problem of measurement

It is worth considering the problem of setting objectives or targets where measurement is difficult. This should not prevent objectives being set. Most jobs have some aspects that can be pinned down. For example, if you ask a personnel office to keep the handbooks up to date (objective – 'issue revised pages within five days of receipt of a new agreement' or 'reach agreement on deputizing by the end of October' for example), you ensure that the job has an operational focus. In addition, if part of the job is tightly and explicitly measured, the vigour that is generated will in any case impact on other parts of the job where measurement is less easy. Nevertheless this is not so easy to deal with where a reward performance system is established. Clearly it is important that all managers are treated as fairly as possible and in respect of payment it would be unfair if one manager's performance targets were demonstrably easier to achieve than another's. These problems are discussed in Chapter 7.

Productivity

The textbooks tell you that there are two extremes of schemes that are tried from time to time in various companies. At one end of the scale payment by results (PBR) systems directly relate pay to work done. (These are the work-studied incentive payment (WSIP) schemes.) At the other end overall performance is measured and all employees receive an average reward.

Of course, for a bonus scheme to be successful, an employee must be able to influence earning power directly and the employer must be sure of getting the output required. But for these to be possible, you have to implement even tighter and more complex control mechanisms which then make the production–reward connection tenuous! Thus bonus systems have within them the seeds of their own destruction. It is not surprising therefore that there is a constant ebbing and flowing of remeasurement, revision, control, weakening, emerging slackness, remeasurement and so on. It was ironic to notice that in 1986 Leyland Vehicles bought out their quality bonus because of complex control problems, while Austin Rover negotiated *in* a quality bonus! There are other inevitable problems. In many organizations it will be impossible to isolate the bonus receivers from other employees. As a result bonus earnings are not allowed to escalate because the company wants to preserve differentials with supervisors and managers and reduce the potential for abuse.

The problem is that a 'manual' WSIP scheme makes the company vulnerable to claims of unfairness in that one group of employees is singled out to have fluctuating earnings. The company then falls into the next trap. 'Ah,' they say, 'but do not worry, earnings don't fluctuate all that much anyway.' To which the response is 'OK, then annual salaries and no bonus will not be a problem!'

There is a payments paradox here for which many organizations are seeking an answer. Many hugely successful companies see no value in WSIP schemes and will not touch them. However, in HR terms it is important to ensure that a solution is proposed that would work in a particular company with its own supervisors and other managers and with its own employees. If they are used to a WSIP environment then change is more difficult and the simple removal of such schemes may result in a fall in productivity and an increase in production and running costs. The debate is therefore about the maintenance of performance and an annual salary without bonus.

There is one further point. We have to recognize that bonus schemes work best for self-contained tasks with a clearly defined work content. This is relatively easy if you regard the task, for example, as selling a microwave. However, if the company thinks that quality of service and courtesy are crucial then the position is more difficult. This is because service and courtesy are less easy to grasp as concepts. This is particularly difficult because a customer will identify his or her own view of what service is. Perhaps if a company plans to take service and customers seriously, then it will be necessary to establish new ways of monitoring and paying for productivity.

Performance and development appraisal

In order to ensure that objectives are being met and individual performance standards are being achieved, the organization needs some method of checking and discussing performance. A survey (Institute of Personnel Management 1986) suggested that in the UK 82 per cent of employers operate some type of performance appraisal scheme. The non-users were not just the smaller companies where close-knit working relationships made formal appraisals less necessary. It was apparent in the survey that many large organizations, particularly in UK public administration, operated no formal mechanism to identify objectives and check on performance.

The appraisal also provides the framework in which the individual's objectives and performance criteria are set for the coming period. At the same time any strengths or problem areas will be identified and dealt with or at least suggestions and proposals made for their resolution. The assessment of potential is also an important part of the individual review process. Many companies (over 70 per cent according to the IPM survey) believe that potential can be assessed using the judgements of managers gained at the time of review. It is an important part of the process because the organization needs to be sure that employees of sufficient quality are available. In human resourcing, quality people are recognized as a prerequisite for quality goods and services. As a consequence human resourcing will focus more on quality people and their identification than might have been the case in traditional personnel management.

Linking development, appraisal and objectives

Returning again to the IPM survey, Figure 6.3 shows how this confirmed the reasons companies gave for reviewing performance. Development considerations such as assessing training and career moves were highly placed. Also important was performance and its review and agreeing and setting of objectives for the ensuing period. It seems essential therefore that the review system adopted within an organization should cover all those aspects. There will be those who believe that development especially should be separate from appraisal. But setting objectives, appraising their achievement and dealing with problems is a central theme of planning for the effective use of human resources. It is impossible to think of these three aspects being separated in any way – they are inter-related. The actual achievement of development targets (as opposed to their identification) can be regarded more properly as an aspect of education, training and development and this area is discussed in Chapter 3.

	%
To assess training and development needs	97
To help improve current performance	97
To review past performance	98
To assess future potential/promotability	71
To assist career planning decisions	75
To set performance objectives	81
To assess increases to new levels in salary	40
Others – eg updating personnel records	4

Source: Hogg March 1988

Figure 6.3   Why Companies Review Performance

Salary decisions

There is, however, a received wisdom in the personnel field that salary decisions should not be connected with the development-performance-appraisal review. This is stated (Harper 1987) as one of the most frequent causes of failure and dissatisfaction in such schemes. It is argued that this arises from the impossibility of marrying up a system which is primarily aimed at providing information for a salary review with a system which is intended to improve current performance (Torrington and Hall 1987).

The difficulty has long been discussed and the vote has clearly come down against integrating salary and performance/appraisal/ development reviews. The arguments are obvious – people will be less likely to discuss their weaknesses and be open about problems if they perceive a direct follow through to their performance reward. Nothing is as important as salary.

I recognize the overwhelming support for this view but I would argue that salary *should* be an integral feature. The problems of a lack of openness are real but they should be considerably lessened in an HR environment. If employees are treated with respect and allowed to maintain their personal integrity, the fears that lead to concealment of problems will be lessened. In addition, the rigorous setting and measuring of objectives means that failures will be obvious. There will be little purpose in pretending they do not exist.

Even worse, the separation of salary issues is, in any case, fraud. People should be rewarded for good performance and should know what is expected and how they will be assessed. To pretend that such decisions will not directly impact on a salary and promotion review is deceitful.

The failure to make the link may also be wrong. Salary (along with promotion) is the clearest, loudest statement that an organization makes about an employee's status. At the moment of making a salary award one employee is separated from another. This is like selection for promotion. No one likes having to tell the unsuccessful candidate and feel their sense of bitter disappointment. Of course people do not like to link the process with performance reviews – they do not like the process at all! The problems with salary in performance reviews are the problems of telling a person that someone else is more highly valued. No one likes to be told that and no one likes doing the telling.

In terms of planning for human resources I believe that it will pay dividends to face people frankly. People should be told, 'I am sorry, I paid her more because I value her performance more highly', or 'I am sorry, he is better than you.' They can be let down gently but they should not be misled. In practice the truth is avoided. The manager says, 'If it had been up to me . . .' or 'You are too valuable to me here' or 'Your chance is coming with such and such a job.' In these ways we seek to conceal our true views of people from them. In fact employees also play the avoidance game by blaming their failure to be promoted on 'office politics'. This is discussed further in Chapter 14.

Interestingly Figure 6.3 identifies 40 per cent of companies as using performance reviews to assess salary and this is suggested as being on the increase (Hogg March 1988). Perhaps this is one of those cases when the academics and professionals are failing to keep pace with new ideas and concepts. We shall see!

Performance and development review for all

The essential nature of HR is to encourage the application of common conditions to all employees. It follows from this that all employees should be assessed, have opportunities for development, have clear objectives and be involved in the process. The traditional practice of limiting the development and performance review procedures to senior employees is not realistic or right. HR requires that all employees contribute to corporate objectives and therefore all have to have open to them facilities for personal development. Of course such development cannot be wasted (a training course should only be given where it is relevant to the employee) and therefore an essential prerequisite is the integration of development with performance setting and assessment.

Links to teamwork and commitment

The importance of performance, objectives and appraisal reviews to teamwork and commitment cannot be stressed too strongly. Indeed it is through knowing what the job is about and where it is going that a sense of direction and purpose is gained. This in turn leads to the development of team-work and commitment.

Human resourcing is not a series of separate activities. It is very much an integration of personnel practices aimed at customers, quality and people. Everything should be directed to those ends.

Assessment and selection centres

Given the focus on development and performance and the recognition of the subjectivity of interviews and reviews, organizations are increasingly looking to new methods. Assessment centres have a number of possible uses, such as:

- assessing performance
- identifying behavioural strengths and weaknesses
- identifying development needs
- assessing potential
- allowing cross-company comparisons
- selecting candidates for promotion.

There are many different approaches and many consultants who offer their services. The advice given appears to concentrate on the wisdom of tailoring schemes to particular companies and (part of this) of keeping the consultants as advisers not executives. It is also possible to automate the processes somewhat by the use of tests and self-scoring techniques. (Rodger and Mabey 1987.)

Although assessment centres, or development centres (DC) as they are also called, have been used previously for background development identification, the emphasis on human resourcing has resulted in the integration of the processes with selection procedures. Thus, the centre is used in different but linking ways. Clearly the nearer the process is to job selection, the more participants will try and adopt different approaches, which may result in reducing development benefits.

A fear of forms

The final plea should be to watch the growth of paper. Many organizations appear to believe that if managers are not committed to the development and performance appraisal process, any problems can be overcome by forcing them to fill in boxes on endless sheets of paper. What matters is attitude and no amount of form-filling will overcome an attitude problem. Managers and employees have to be committed to the process. This will be greatly assisted if the recommendations and results are acted upon. Nothing will more completely destroy confidence and create a cynical response than a failure to carry out promises. Suggestions that it is possible to do away with forms altogether sound unlikely, although ideas have been put forward. (Pryor and Mayo 1985, Institute of Personnel Management 1986, Anderson, 1987.)

Summary

Having clear objectives both for the organization and the employee are at the heart of a human resourcing approach. In turn it is essential that the extent of the achievement of these objectives is assessed through a performance review process. This process should highlight any problems and therefore the development needs of the employee. At the same time it becomes possible to set new objectives for a new period. The organization has, however, to resolve the place of salary review, particularly if attempts are made to link performance to reward. It is necessary to ensure that company policy and practice (the stated policy and the done policy) are in line. Good objectives are extremely important in performance and productivity, and both the problems and the benefits of WSIP schemes need to be looked at. Development and performance reviews should be provided for all staff, and the possible use of assessment centres should be considered.

Chapter 7
Reward Management

The concept of reward management

The focus on HRM has brought with it a serious questioning of traditional views of payment. First the terms themselves have been scrutinized and then changed. So the bland 'payment administration' has lost ground to talk of 'remuneration' and 'compensation'. These words have in turn begun to lose their popularity – remuneration because it is only a jargon-type substitute for 'payment' and compensation because it gives too much of an impression that the company is making amends for the punishment of having to come to work!

Reward management has been criticized (Torrington and Hall 1987) as suggesting a special payment for a special act. Perhaps that is the thrust behind HRM – is the company not looking for wholehearted commitment, where each day is new, exciting and fun? One criticism of reward management is the 'old wine in new bottles' argument. As this chapter will show, much of what is developing under the HRM umbrella is new, but even if it were not there is nothing wrong with the personnel manager remarketing the profession and perhaps creating new interest in the process. Other terms such as 'pay' are limiting in what they cover. 'Reward' correctly conjures up a reference to the whole job and its conditions, of which pay is part – albeit an important part. For these reasons 'reward management' is considered more appropriate in HR terms.

Fairness and reward management

The phrase 'a fair day's work for a fair day's pay' has long existed in the personnel manager's repertoire. One problem has always been that one person's definition of fairness is not necessarily shared by others. Fairness in questions of reward has been further confused by attempts to apply Marxist collectivism. Marxism saw no problem in failing to recognize different levels of contribution. The creed was 'from each according to his ability; to each according to his need'. The simple attractiveness of such a slogan blinded a generation of personnel managers. The logical conclusion would be equal payment for all, a cause few would have found either attractive or workable.

HRM recognizes that equality is nonsense in the way it has been typically expressed. The criterion for HR is that employees should be *free* to achieve within their own capabilities and that for that achievement the company should establish *fair* procedures for reward management. (The absurdity of the equality craze in the face of the obvious evidence that in the crucial matter of their basic attributes people are not equal, is referred to again in Chapter 10.)

The freedom to achieve refers to the opportunity to undergo education and training programmes or to have personally oriented development programmes. These are dealt with in Chapter 3. The present concern is the establishment of fairness in reward management.

The felt-fair concept

The question of fairness is usually applied to an internal reference point. The position is slightly more complicated with the growing introduction of legislation requiring employers to avoid discrimination on grounds of race, sex, religion or (in the USA) age.

External references to fairness do not have the same meaning because no personal contract exists with people who are not already associated with the company. Consequently, external references to fair pay levels are usually expressed in terms of market-relatedness. In turn the pressure on the company is to determine whether rewards are sufficient to attract and retain people of the required calibre and qualifications and therefore whether it is *sensible* to continue underpaying (or indeed overpaying!) compared with other employers.

This internal–external concept can perhaps be explained by reference to an example from the teaching profession. A school may wonder whether it is *sensible* to, say, underpay physics and maths teachers to such an extent that they seek better-paid careers elsewhere. This is a question of market forces.

If it is decided to pay more for physics teachers the governors will then be faced with an internal question of *fairness*, namely, is it fair in the same school to pay a graduate physics or maths teacher more than a graduate home economics teacher, simply because one is in short supply and the other is not?

The solution to such problems is to be found in the 'felt-fair' concept. The concept is unusual in personnel jargon in that the words describe what is meant! Felt-fair is simply that which employees and the organization generally and mutually feel to be fair. This will refer to both *absolute levels of pay* (Is the whole reward package fair?) and to *relative differentials* (Am I paid sufficiently more than my junior?). Felt-fair is attributed to Jacques (in Fox 1972) and since he wrote in detail about it in the 1960s it has proved remarkably durable.

Criteria for fairness in reward management

The HR manager is therefore aware of the need to ensure that the reward package is fair and sensible. There is a clear need to plan for the achievement of company and employee support. These plans will be directed at a number of reward areas such as absolute pay levels, internal differentials, merit systems, bonus/commission schemes and market conditions.

Absolute pay levels

Employees obviously have a keen interest in what they earn. The HR manager recognizes that to many companies it has not been clear that the reward package is a personal symbol of worth that can be paraded to the outside world as well as internally.

To the employee *purchasing power* is important. The benefits received in cash and in kind will significantly determine the standard of living for the employee and his or her family. Even 'second-income' jobs are important in this consideration of purchasing power. Dickens's Mr Micawber knew that the difference between happiness and misery was a shilling in £20 – marginal income is therefore very important.

The expectation gap

Concepts of fairness in absolute pay levels are affected in a variety of ways. Purchasing power is an important consideration but is not the only one. Reference to external factors may result in employees seeing that their *relative* position is declining or increasing. The organization will gladly accept the benefits of an increase in relative pay levels and will have therefore also to accept the problems of a relative decline.

Comparisons with other employees are not the only criteria. The strength of the company and its ability to pay is another important factor. Employees working for a successful company will expect to share in that success.

Internal relativities

HR managers will often find that problems of internal relativities are the most time-consuming and the hardest to resolve. They are also the most crucial. An organization can to some extent choose its external comparators and the level at which it wishes to pitch earnings, and this is discussed later. This is not true of internal relativities – if they are wrong the organization will suffer and the effects will be rapid.

This will happen for two reasons. First, the employee and the company will have more accurate information on which to base a judgement when considering internal relativities. Secondly, and more important, people are more affected by the irritant that is closer to them than the one which is some way off.

External comparisons are important but the priority for HRM is to get the internal relativities right. If employees' perception of felt-fair are negative, it will usually be in the area of internal relativities that solutions are to be found.

Job evaluation

In Britain the notion of job evaluation was given an enormous push in the mid-1960s. The Labour government's National Board for Prices and Incomes made job evaluation the basis for assessing pay as increases in pay could, by law, only be awarded for an increase in responsibility. It was perhaps unfortunate that, for the British, job evaluation had such a political birth.

Clearly the organization needs some method of systematically establishing internal relativities between the levels of responsibility of various jobs, which can then be used as a basis for determining pay levels. Unfortunately the theory can mar the practice as job evaluation becomes the master and not the servant of management.

One problem is that to preserve the integrity of the system there is a tendency to demand more and more detail about jobs. What can start as a good discipline for managers – that they should work out what a job is about – can quickly become a charade as jobs and duties are manipulated to achieve a magic points score and therefore the pay level that is sought.

Systematic not scientific

It is essential for the fundamental weakness of job evaluation to be recognized. Its proponents often refer to it being 'scientific' or, less grandly, 'objective'. It is neither, particularly in its original design, where the selection of factors is inevitably largely based on values. Job evaluation is systematic. Its purpose is to provide an accepted framework in which pay levels can be determined.

The problem comes when this basic framework is *not* generally accepted, and under attack the system is applied more rigidly. No amount of stylized job descriptions, jargon and trend lines can conceal the fact that job evaluation is value-laden. The point is no more than to provide a procedure to assess and establish those values in a systematic way.

It is people not jobs that count

One fundamentally wrong conclusion that underlies much thinking in the field of job evaluation is that the job is the subject not the person. This tendency is understandable. The infinite variety of human behaviour means that the constant factor – the job – is the subject of evaluation. The problems arise when the process stops there, with a pretence that people do not count. In HR terms this is not only wrong but is also contrary to what is intended. The objective is to release the creativity that for many employees remains locked within them or channelled towards other activities. The HR belief is that people alter jobs. Many companies might endure this as an inevitable by-product of employing people instead of machines. The HR company not only *expects* people to alter jobs but *hopes* that they will do so. Dynamic growth is a key to HR. Unfortunately it does not rest easily with the stifling bureaucracy of many job evaluation schemes.

Lack of flexibility

From the point of view of the HR manager the worst problems of a job evaluation system are liable to come from a lack of flexibility. The search for detail in jobs to establish minute differences is the antithesis of HRM, where the emphasis is on multi-skill jobs, few job titles and interchangeability. Job evaluation encourages differentiation between jobs, while HRM wants to embrace those differences into levels of people at work.

There are few job titles and the fewest number of managerial layers possible. Some companies have reduced all tasks from managing director to manufacturing staff to a handful of titles, but in 1988 Ford UK had a major strike trying to reduce its *manufacturing* levels down to 48.

The HR emphasis is therefore to broaden jobs to get people to think of themselves as an engineer, rather than as a maintenance, electrical, operations or any other kind of engineer, or as a clerk rather than a filing clerk, registry clerk, wages clerk, accounts clerk and so on. This question of titles is not trivial. Once people are separated they are likely to become defensive of their specialist role. The British are particularly adept at this, though territorial disputes arising from jobs also exist elsewhere.

A future for job evaluation

It is not possible or desirable to eliminate job evaluation entirely. The HR-based organization requires a system to look at differentials and relativities like any other. The crucial need is to ensure that the system is not *over-detailed*, encouraging the separations and divisions which destroy flexibility and with it the ability to change. Multi-skill jobs should be an inherent part of the system.

The job evaluation manager must also be wary of references to training in job descriptions. Training and development is a continuous flowing and updating process. It is not a badge to be achieved and that's the end of it. Rapid and technological change necessitates continuous training.

The elimination of sex and race bias is another important objective of job evaluation. Felt-fair may be unfair (and illegal) if it is based on past values and assessments which had some sex and race bias integral to them. Such values will not be acceptable in an HR environment – women must not be steered away from 'men's jobs' and the evaluation process must not reinforce what is wrong.

Finally, the solution to territorial disputes between managers over pay lies not only in the acceptance of an evaluation system but in the recognition that strong central control is needed. There will be differences because people alter jobs. These differences should not be allowed to develop in an arbitrary and uncontrolled way. Central control can avoid that happening. The wrong solution is an imposed rigidity that fears variety lest it should spread. Variety is essential in an HR environment and can be provided through a reward system which has elements of performance and merit recognition.

The reward manager's role

As I have said above, human nature being what it is, it is unlikely that there will be ready agreement about relativities and special awards. For this reason reward management requires the same strong central control necessary for successful job evaluation. It is not possible to leave managers to make decisions about their own people except within clearly defined boundaries.

Frankly this creates a difficulty. Managers' need for specialized advice has not escaped the notice of consultants. Such people have a strong interest in promoting complex reward structures and they will not be slow in recommending them. The company has to reflect on the extent to which the advice it is receiving is as independent as is claimed.

Grading structures and merit schemes

The pay system a company adopts tells one a lot about that company's philosophy. A company that has uniform salary tables with little or no room for individual reward believes in collectivism rather than individual creativeness. On the other hand one that values initiative will ensure that it has a system to reward and therefore reinforce that initiative.

There are other issues of pay which in many companies are relatively low-key – merit and reward for achieving objectives. Of course, merit pay relates crucially to performance, objectives and appraisal, which is discussed in more detail in Chapter 6. The main observation at this point is that the manager should question whether the traditional grading structures still common in many companies are the best way to organize pay, particularly at the senior managerial levels.

The grades usually apply to everyone in a particular job – paying more to a high achiever is virtually impossible. Furthermore, you are rewarded for attendance and service, not for creativity and achievement. This is shown when you consider the criteria for climbing up the grades. (Actually 'climbing' is the wrong word; the process is so automatic that 'progressing' is more appropriate!)

For a managerial reward system to be effective there are a number of criteria which must be met, namely:

- Be clear about what you expect to achieve.
- Get the support of senior management.
- Ensure that employees see the system as fair.

This leads on to questions of recruitment, retention and motivation. How you intend to reward individuals and groups within the same system is a difficulty to be faced. It is essential to consider the non-monetary factors such as cars and mobility perks. Finally, there has to be a debate about how much of an employee's salary should be performance-related, and whether the base salary is 100 per cent (with the good performer receiving 120 per cent) or whether the average performer should receive 80 per cent with the rest as an incentive.

Anyone who favours merit systems needs to think very hard about what they mean. There will be some injustice and a great deal of effort involved. Remember, if you work in an organization which is willing to let you make off-hand, ill-prepared decisions about the people who work for you, then you can be sure that it will let someone else treat *you* the same way! Therefore you have to have controls external to the function, formal procedures, development reviews, appraisals and frank talking. The prize of enhancing the performance–reward relationship is worth it – but the effort involved is formidable.

You also have to accept that people doing jobs bearing similar titles will not necessarily get the same pay. You must look at what is important to you and how you will reward it.

The HR company is concerned with developing initiative, creativity and individual decision-making. In such an environment a merit-based or oriented system of reward is essential.

It is taken for granted that other aspects of management are measured and levels of performance determined. So sales per square metre, share price-earnings ratio, return on capital, capital utilization, turnover as percentage of stock and so on can all be used. It seems natural that people's performance should be similarly assessed. This assessment is discussed in Chapter 6. The issue here is the extent to which it should determine levels of reward.

What is performance-related pay? It is the linking of *strategic performance* measured *over a period of time* with some *tangible reward* (usually money) which is withheld if the required performance is not achieved. The reference to strategic performance and measurement over a period of time is important. Rewards based on the tactical completion of specific tasks are more properly considered as piecework or work-studied approaches and not as merit-based reward systems of the type envisaged in reward management. Of course piecework and work-studied systems have a place and they will be referred to later. In reward management the issue is less about the tactics of task completion (sell six cars this week) but more about strategic achievement of objectives (achieve *x* sales as a percentage of capital in the first quarter).

For these reasons merit and performance management often has more relevance at the strategic managerial level of the company and less at the tactical operating level. The clerk working on routine tasks has a shorter time-span of discretion than a chief executive (and therefore less ability to affect the organization strategically). This concept follows through into reward management. The greater the time-span of a post the more relevant will be strategic targets and their achievement.

Clearly in extreme cases (very low performers being removed or high performers being moved on early) there would be general agreement on how they should be handled. The real questions are whether larger numbers of employees should have an element of their pay fixed by a merit system; and, if so, how great that element should be.

Nature of the organization

One aspect relates to the type of organization under consideration. Merit systems might be more appropriate in executive, initiative-oriented companies such as hi-tech, sales and marketing or others subject to rapid change. A merit system may be less applicable in a stable and mature bureaucracy where consistency and the giving of advice, rather than executive problem solving, is at a premium. It is a mistake to think that merit systems are universally applicable.

Nature of the work

The work undertaken by the employee will have a significant effect on the prospects for merit pay. This is because not all work is easily measured, especially cerebral effort. For example a sales manager's performance might easily be measured but how would you reward a solicitor? The problem of how to handle jobs where specific and measurable targeting is difficult can cause the merit system to fail if as a result it leads to favouritism, looseness and a consequent lack of credibility.

In addition, routine work (particularly clerical) does not have clear performance separators. There is at lower hierarchical levels less room for the initiative that is to be encouraged or rewarded. There is also more room for manipulation by sacrificing quality for output. For this reason it is generally found that organizations seeking variable pay through merit systems operate them differently at different levels of the hierarchy. At the clerical level, systems may well be group-based. Of course in a group there is less prospect of individual effort affecting performance and therefore there is no motivation through individual reward.

Extent of variable pay

Given a desire to develop a merit system how much of the reward package should be variable, ie dependent on achieving an established performance criterion? Where a scheme is poorly defined and group based there is little point in having a significant variable pay element. In this case pay variations are small – often between 2½ and 5 per cent.

Of course where it is possible to establish individual targets over a period it is possible to have a greater variable element. Clearly the amount must be sufficient to make a difference – so something over 5 per cent (after inflation) is a minimum. At the top end the employee will be reluctant to be exposed to significant variability, which could result in insecurity arising from unstable earnings. For this reason 20 per cent might be a maximum. Many companies (Armstrong and Murlis 1988) appear to find 10–15 per cent acceptable and workable.

The principles of merit pay

There are a number of important principles which must be followed and these are shown in Figure 7.1.

Fairness is extremely important. It is no good having a system which rewards some people more easily than others. For this reason control is crucial. Central control is the second prerequisite for success. There must be a controlling function which ensures that departmental targets are set with equal rigour and that merit awards are made fairly. Central control also involves ensuring that related aspects such as performance appraisals are held at agreed intervals.

Fairness perceived by all
Central control by the HR function
Performance targets defined in advance
Acceptable targets
Understood performance system
Clear, definable and understood performance targets
Reasonable base pay level

Figure 7.1   Principles of Merit Pay

This is a big role for the HR function and one which will not endear it to line management colleagues! This does not minimize the role of the line function. Only that function will be able to express company objectives meaningfully in terms of performance targets.

It is important that a merit system is supported by a generally understood system of performance appraisal and target setting. The first principle of fairness also makes it important that everyone knows what the rules are and is experienced in their application. It follows that performance target setting must precede a merit pay system. If this is done with care the worst fears of employees will be allayed.

Clear performance targets are important, since the purpose of a merit system is to encourage the achievement of targets and to reinforce a culture that sets store by high performance. The problem will be to try and set targets for performance in measurable terms. In practice though, despite the fears that some jobs are not amenable to clear targeting, this is rarely found to be a key factor where schemes fail. It is of course taken for granted that targets must be *set* in advance, following discussion, and if not agreed are at least acceptable to the persons involved.

It is important that the guaranteed base pay is set at the appropriate level. As has been indicated earlier the felt-fair focus will be on internal rather than external relativities. If internal relativities are seen as out of balance, injustices will exist and people will manipulate the system to overcome them (for example by setting easy targets or by controlling them loosely). This is not to say that external relativities are unimportant but that their importance lies in market sector positioning over a longer period. Generally there is more room for error in external imbalance than internal.

Internal differentials can be established by reference to a method of evaluation. External differentials can be set informally by reference to job advertisements in the press (if a salary is quoted), but more systematically by company membership of 'wages clubs' or external wage surveys. A number of consultant organizations offer such a service and allow comparisons of salary levels in subscribing companies.

Causes of failure in reward systems

There are a number of problems that lead to the failure of pay-performance systems. A key problem is that in order to be effective the employee must be able to influence performance and thereby increase the reward. However, to ensure that real added value is achieved there is a need for control. To overcome the avoidance of this control and the manipulation of the scheme, more detailed and complex control mechanisms are established. In turn this leads to an emphasis on mechanics and controls and the gradual separation of performance from pay. Such factors have led to many piecework schemes being dropped, so there is a paradox and many WSIP/ piecework schemes appear to have within them the seeds of their own destruction. Interestingly these problems can occur equally with managerial merit systems – it is just that the history is shorter and less clearly set out in the textbooks.

There is a further problem. The theory behind piecework and WSIP schemes is that harder effort is rewarded by higher pay and therefore the added value of the extra output is returned in part to the employee in a bonus. It is not so obvious that this actually occurs in practice. Very quickly the payment of a certain bonus level becomes the standard and management and employees try to ensure that earnings are maintained. This is done by allowing schemes to become out of date, by loose control, by judicious use of the pen in bonus returns and so on. This problem is worse in merit systems, where the connection between performance and added value is not always clear, particularly at more senior levels. There is a risk that again the salary plus merit pay will be seen as the base salary. In any event, pay can only come from one source. Unless added value is achieved the merit system simply adds to employment costs. When that happens, the company will be tempted to manipulate pay by positioning at, say, the upper quartile rather than the upper decile, which might in fact be affordable. Then the difference between the upper quartile and upper decile is paid in a merit form – thus nothing is given to the employee beyond what was available anyway.

Finally, there is a continuous need to update the mechanisms. Many organizations will tell you (privately!) that their much-vaunted appraisal and performance targeting systems have a tendency to atrophy. Very quickly financial pressures are exerted which mean that the system is manipulated and control is lost. The textbooks will say this is a function of sterility in the management of the process. No insider will admit to flaws in the system, such as lack of objectivity, the need to change targets in response to pressures, the mutuality amongst employees which means that failure is not identified and plain simple inertia!

Payment by results

The role of payment by results schemes in relation to increasing production is discussed in Chapter 6. Here the concern is with the use of such systems as motivations within the sphere of reward management.

There is some superficial similarity between a merit system as described above and PBR systems. However, a merit system relates to general performance measured against a few targets over a period of time. PBR systems are based on tactical task completion often broken down into tasks lasting from a few minutes to a few hours. This is a crucial difference. Of course the fundamental paradox still exists – the need is for a linking of performance with reward but the ever-increasing complexity of management and control results in a tenuous if not broken link and the payment system ceases to be the motivator it is intended to be. A PBR scheme will not motivate employees if they cannot influence the amount of pay received. For this reason, company-wide added value schemes, or even those affecting large groups within a company, do not increase performance in a direct and tactical way.

WSIP and piecework schemes have other problems but many are associated with difficulties of control. The increasing complexity of documentation needed to control payment, along with detailed and fine measurement, places the emphasis on form rather than task completion.

From an HR viewpoint there are more serious problems with PBR schemes. The emphasis on task completion inevitably values more highly the tasks that can be identified, measured and timed. So maintaining a car is a question of timing, of nuts and bolts, of replacing filters and the rest. The problem is that in HR terms, important though those aspects are, the real job is customer satisfaction and cost control. PBR systems see those as effects not causes, they are what follows from task completion, not the task itself. The HR philosophy is very much the reverse – customers and people come first (they are the reason for the organization's existence) and everything else follows from that. Those who have travelled on some public transport systems or stayed in some hotels know what happens when the customer/person–task focus is reversed.

There is another serious defect with PBR systems. They become a substitute for control by management. Indeed PBR is introduced in many companies because the company has little confidence in the ability of its supervisors to control the work its employees are undertaking.

There is, in addition, a deeper concern. This is the extent to which a PBR system is seen by employees as an insult to them. This will happen if employees draw the conclusion that they are not trusted to manage and organize their own work.

There are other problems. For example, if the base rate of pay is depressed to allow for the bonus element, a conspiracy is likely between managers and employees to ensure that employees are assured the maximum bonus. This process suggests that time-consuming and bureaucratic as remeasurement processes may be, it is doubtful whether PBR schemes can be kept up to date. Whatever the true level of success, maintenance and remeasurement absorbs a great deal of time and managerial effort. Where there is a heavy trade union involvement the process is lengthened and perhaps politicized.

The personnel manager has long suspected that PBR schemes are based on a mechanical view of the job that does not work in practice. This dissatisfaction is expressed in many ways, often by companies continually seeking to move from one scheme type to another.

From an HR point of view there is another reservation. PBR systems are best suited to manual rather than office work. Most systems are therefore directed towards manual employees. In the UK (though less so in the US and Europe and apparently not at all in major employers in Japan) these are often hourly-based weekly-paid employees. This is a fundamental divergence from a key tenet of HRM – the common treatment of employees and the avoidance of arbitrary and outdated, often status-based, separators.

Nevertheless the problems of PBR systems will continue. If an organization is unable to sustain management control, the vacuum created by the loss of PBR will result in a drop in performance and employee abuse of a new-found freedom. At the same time if PBR payments are not guaranteed to employees, their income will fall, with consequences for morale and resignation rates. It is clear therefore that disengagement from PBR may be desirable but not straightforward and not achievable without careful preparation, perhaps over a period of years. This preparation will involve action or training and development of supervisors and employees, as well as the substitution of performance control mechanisms and work appraisal and reviews to ensure that productivity does not fall and unit costs rise. Incidentally a revitalized work study function will have a crucial role to play in the establishment of control mechanisms which support but do not rule managers and employees in their work.

Beyond the fringe

A discussion of payments cannot be complete without reference to the fringe benefit. In practice fringe benefits distort relativities and give a false impression of actual reward if not properly accounted for. Apart from this obvious defect there are other, even worse, aspects that affect the organization in an HR context.

First, fringe benefits are divisive. The benefit to one employee is quickly sought by others, particularly if it is not clearly earmarked for a particular purpose. The tendency towards rigidity is another serious defect. Employees with a fringe benefit may be reluctant to move to another job or an associated company if the fringe is lost.

A further difficulty is the complexity caused to the reward structure. Employees and managers become confused by the benefits, which prevent a clear, powerful message being transmitted. It is crucial in an HR environment that the message of what behaviour and importance is rewarded in what way is simple to understand, otherwise it is lost and the link between reward and effort becomes tenuous. It could be more serious if the confusion leads to the reinforcement of wrong behaviour patterns or to certain jobs or locations in a company being sought out because of the fringe benefits available there.

These aspects have led many people (Skae 1988) to seek a return to 'clean cash' supported by merit and performance awards. Of course some benefits would properly continue. For example the home-based education of peripatetic expatriate employees' children would in many circumstances be essential (eg diplomatic staff or construction engineers). Finally, it would appear that the company car, at least in the UK, is a permanent fixture unless the Inland Revenue taxes it beyond endurance, when cash would then become preferable. If the car remains then it should be allocated with more rationality than has been the case in many organizations in the past.

Summary

HR management recognizes that creativity and performance achievement are crucial to organizational success. One key way of reinforcing creativity and performance achievement is to reward it. Merit systems, particularly at more senior levels, covering less routine tasks are an important part of a strategy for reward management. Methods of determining internal differentials can be assisted by job evaluation but the methods available appear to have serious disadvantages

Whatever approaches to reward management are chosen, central control and continuous review will be essential to guard against abuse, sterility and inertia.

Chapter 8

Creating and Communicating with Teams

The differences between HR and industrial relations

There are important differences of approach between HR and IR. Industrial relations deals less with employees as individual people and more with the processes and procedures which regulate the terms and conditions of their employment. That is one important difference, for the proper central theme for human resourcing is people and not procedures. A second important point is the tendency, frequently the imperative, to operate industrial relations within a short time horizon. Human resource planning implies a long time horizon.

There will be organizations where industrial relations as it is typically thought of (short-term, combative, manipulative, fire-fighting etc) does not apply. This would be where relations with trade unions had been established in a particular and constructive way. More commonly, the lack of industrial relations is found in organizations where trade unions either are not recognized or do not have sufficient membership to justify being taken seriously.

In short, therefore, employee relations in an HR environment is seen as intitiative-taking while industrial relations has traditionally been seen as reactive. There is no reason why this is inevitable and there are many organizations in which industrial relations has an increasingly strategic employee-oriented view running through it – these things do not fit into the neat and clearly defined boxes that authors would like to ascribe to them! There is also no reason why trade unions should cast themselves in the reactive role – indeed if the trade unions ever become initiating, rather than reactive, organizations, then there are many reluctant managers who might find it difficult to cope. For the present however, despite some examples to the contrary, the trade unions generally prefer to resist the word processor rather than to castigate management for failing to propose its extension. Trade union issues are dealt with in more detail in Chapter 9.

The objectives of employee relations

Recognizing that differences exist between industrial relations and HR, what are the criteria for success and the means of achieving that success in an employee relations strategy? An outline is shown in Figure 8.1. The overall objective of the human resource strategy is the achievement of committed employees and this is done by the development of integrated teams led by a supervisor. The ideal would be employees working in harmony with the company and its objectives, which of course will include the wider community interest. The employee relations strategy plays a key part in achieving committed employees both at the personal and the organizational level through building confidence in the organization and its managers.

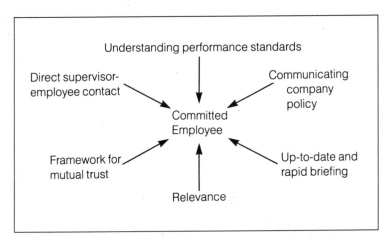

Figure 8.1   An HR Employee Relations Strategy

Communicating understanding, not information

The importance of communications has been stressed so frequently for so many years it is perhaps worth pausing to reflect why the expected achievements have not been forthcoming. This is perhaps a result of the same problems that hamper much that is good in personnel management generally – namely the reliance on a centralized and bureaucratic approach that emphasizes the technical and rational at the expense of humanity and feelings. The risk with communication is that the process and style will become more important than the content. This is presumably what Marshall McLuhan the North American sociologist was referring to when he said that 'the medium is the message'.

This is perhaps exemplified in the house magazine and the company video. These two vehicles of communication are much loved by the senior vice-president of the corporation. A great deal of effort and expense is lavished on polished productions. But are they relevant to an employee relations strategy aimed at communicating understanding rather than information? Returning to Figure 8.1 it can be seen that both magazine and video fail on a number of the criteria referred to. It is impossible to be up to date and fast in communicating through magazines and videos. Any attempt to do so would result in a loss of polish or a repetitive style. This would be unacceptable because we are used to seeing glossy magazines and colourful active videos. Any loss of standard to improve immediacy would give the appearance of a second-rate, hastily prepared product. The curious fact is that an employee would willingly accept a typewritten sheet from a supervisor as a means of communication but would be disdainful of the same quality of document purporting to be a house magazine!

The second failing of the magazine and the video is perhaps more important. Any message is better received if it is the supervisor who is giving it; the magazine and video separate the supervisor from the team. It has to be said, therefore, that the magazine and the video have a limited role in any employee relations strategy. The media moguls may not like it but the truth is that a few words between a trusted supervisor and the team will have a thousand times more effect. (Incidentally, in defence of videos, there is no criticism of them as a training tool. They can communicate *information* and back-up discussion can lead to understanding, but this is quite different from the intentions of an employee relations strategy as part of human resource planning.)

How and what to communicate?

Given that the emphasis is on understanding rather than information how should the process be carried out? Building on the importance of the supervisor, the priority should be to use that route. Face-to-face communications are to be greatly preferred. There will, however, be occasions when written messages are required, particularly if it is essential that all employees get the same message at the same time.

The system should not be over-formal. Regular and short sessions are preferable to grand presentations held every six months, though at the corporate level there is room for those also. It is also crucial that they should be two-way affairs. Communication of the one-way 'team briefing' type should by now be a thing of the past. In HR the presumption is that not only do employees *deserve* and *need* to understand but that they have a *contribution* to make. They cannot make that contribution if barriers exist to the proper cross-flows of information.

In terms of content, the subject of communications should be relevant to the employees in their jobs. Therefore the emphasis should be on performance and productivity, supply problems, major customer orders, quality failures and improvements on budgets, profits and sales. This might be developed to include promotions and training (both intended and requested).

All these communications must be a two-way process. With this concentration on the work group the embarrassment of the 'team briefer' inventing things to put in the monthly brief should be avoided.

As a first point, honest replies must be given to questions. This is not easy. There is always a desire in relationships to fudge the issues. Moreover, the failure to act on what is communicated – up or down – will quickly throw the process into disorder and bad repute. Listening is therefore crucial and this means two-way listening like the two-way communication. Only in this manner is there a chance that understanding (two-way!) will result.

Teams and supervisors

From this it can be seen that communication in employee relations should be team-based and supervisor-led. The supervisor is crucial in this as in all aspects of human resource management. The trust and status accorded to the supervisor should be a key objective. It therefore follows that as far as possible communicating should be the supervisor's responsibility. The tests of relevance and immediacy should be achievable. Any information can then be presented in a way that has relevance to the particular group. There is not much point briefing the finer points of London weighting allowances to employees in the company's Welsh factory!

Of course there will be occasions when an exact and specific message has to be communicated to all employees. Such occasions will be few and far between and for day-to-day purposes an informal (but monitored!) process is preferable.

The supervisor–team relationship is at the heart of any communications strategy and maximum effort should be expended in strengthening that bond. The act of communicating is itself a powerful builder. The person who communicates has the power that information brings with it. This in turn requires that the supervisor understands what the objectives are and is willing to carry them out. A cynical supervisor can perhaps do more damage than an effective supervisor can do good!

There are other ways of giving recognition to the supervisor. A key one is his or her role in recruitment and selection. If the team sees new members recruited by other managers it will be obvious to all concerned where the power lies. This will debilitate the supervisor and weaken the bonds in the team she or he leads. The reverse is true if the supervisor plays a part in the interview or assessment and, for example, rings the successful candidate at home the same day with the job offer.

The place is also important. There are occasions when a hotel or conference room is appropriate but the best place is where the team works or prepares for its work. Far too often supervisors separate themselves from such places, and have their own offices some distance away. This is always wrong. These physical barriers to team-building should be removed.

Approaches to building teams

Teams are the pivot of a committed workforce and the central aim of an employee relations strategy within a plan for human resourcing (Belbin 1981). The role of communications has been stressed. An open, honest and frank exchange about the organization's achievements and problems, and the contribution, needs and hopes of employees is a prerequisite for team-building.

There are other factors that are important in an employee relations strategy. The organization will rightly be wary of sending everyone on a team-building course. Such programmes (or 'experiences' as their adherents might prefer to call them!) are widely available. There is no doubt that programmes such as Coverdale, Blakes Grid, T Groups, Total Quality Management, Quality Circles and the rest have an important role to play. But they should be at the end not the start of an employee relations strategy. The consultants selling these team-building services will readily acknowledge the likely causes of failure.

Senior executive support

The most important necessity is the support of a powerful force within the organization. Without this level of commitment it is simply not possible to make the right kind of progress, particularly if significant changes to present organizational values and practices are in prospect. A team-building strategy may show benefits in months but if these benefits are to be other than transitory it is essential that the programme is sustained over a period of time. The effort is likely to be measured in years rather than months. In a way it is indicative of our attitude to employees if we think it could be otherwise. The manager who would readily accept the lengthy time scales involved in setting up a new factory, or even a major revision of computer systems, should not be surprised if an equivalent substantive change in employee attitudes has to be planned and managed over a similar period.

'Them' and 'us' – the antithesis of teams

After the lack of long-term senior executive support perhaps the most frequent cause of regression will be the unwillingness to face up to the barriers that divide managers and employees in the first place.

There was an occasion where a supervisor and an employee were involved in an altercation and the supervisor was dismissed. On appeal the factory group came forth in droves to deny that a fight had taken place. Without evidence the original management decision was reversed on internal appeal and the employee was reinstated. The senior management fretted at the lack of support they had been given. Had they not been undermined and made to look foolish? From a different perspective the situation can be reassessed. The employee work group had shown all the attributes of human beings at their best. The flash of temper had been followed by regret, rallying round, trust and support. This was teamwork in action!

The point is that employees are already in teams. The question is whether the teams are in harmony with the company's purpose. If they are not the result is dysfunctional. The problem for the company in the above case is that they have set themselves against the employees' team.

If the organization writes the agenda in terms of barriers and separation then teams will not flourish. The supervisor will either be an outcast from the work group or will throw her or his lot in with the employees and sink the company.

This is a recurrent problem. Personnel managers have discussed the supervisory problem long and hard over many years. Sociologists have developed a term for the supervisor's predicament. The supervisor has all the conflict of someone occupying the 'boundary role', not sure which side should be the first place of loyalty.

The answer is in the thinking. 'Boundary' implies the line separating one place from another. Not being sure of the 'side' says it all. The organization has allowed separation and division to become the norm – team development is not possible.

The desks and walls that separate supervisors, the executive car parking spaces, the multi-status canteens, the subtle privileges of office are about separating not mutuality. There is absolutely no use in sending people on team-building courses if it is obvious to everyone that on a day-to-day basis teams are discouraged. This does not mean that senior executives are expected to dine with the clerks; in fact the nature of teams is that people will stick with what they perceive as their natural group. The important point is that separation only occurs where it is seen as fair and functional. Guests may well be entertained in a special facility – there is nothing wrong in honouring guests. On a day-to-day basis, however, what justification can there be for one group of employees having access to a finer standard of meat than that available to others? Napoleon for all his aspirations to grandeur ate what his troops ate. Finding it repulsive he acted and invented food preservation by bottling. This shows another useful side-effect of true team-manship – if a person in power experiences bad service some change is likely to occur!

Senior executives have to face the problems of change if teams are to be encouraged. No amount of house magazines, videos, sports and social clubs and team-building courses will effect any change if the attitude in the workplace is based on separation and division. Managers often remark that employees do not listen. In fact the reverse is the case – employees listen very carefully. If I lecture my colleagues about team-work and then stroll to my executive waitress-served lunch while they eat a sandwich on the shop floor then employees know very well what I am saying. They will readily conclude that I do not mean what I say about team-work and will behave accordingly – divisively!

An employee relations strategy will therefore require a thorough review of many traditional aspects of company life. Single-status reviews are becoming increasingly common. Single status is a widespread but not very accurate term. It is obviously wrong to think of a clerk as having the same (single) status as a senior vice-president. What it really means is the harmonization of terms and conditions. A British Institute of Management (BIM) survey (Murlis and Grist 1976) listed the reasons shown in Figure 8.2 for a move to single status. Not referred to explicitly but perhaps as important as those reasons listed is the *moral imperative*. It is extremely difficult to argue over the bargaining table with trade unions that a manual craft employee with 10 years' services should have fewer holidays or less sickness or pension provision than junior office workers who have just walked in through the door. Nevertheless, although there

External Influence	Internal Objective
Social/political climate	To increase employee co-operation
Union pressure	To improve relations
Effect of legislation	To increase productivity
Shortage of unskilled labour	To reduce labour turnover
Foreign influence	To reduce absenteeism To keep down wage bills

Source: Murlis and Grist 1976

Figure 8.2   Reasons for a Move to Single Status

are fewer of them, many companies manage to live with such differences in terms and conditions (even while they are at the same time pressing the virtues of team-work!).

Payments, reward, terms and conditions

The problems created by payments and reward in human resource planning are discussed in Chapter 7. At this point it should be noted that such matters say a great deal about the extent of team building. One obvious source of division is the actual method of payment. In the UK many manual employees are hourly based and weekly paid whereas the staff equivalent will be monthly paid derived from an annual salary. This is an irrelevant hangover from a time where manuals were seen as itinerant and dispensable. (Even worse, recruitment still reflects the prewar mentality of those organizations who advertise 'hands wanted'. These are not people just 'hands'.) The importance of monthly pay and annual salary is that it avoids the contemptuous view of manual employees as temporary and unable to manage their affairs beyond a week at a time.

These aspects are essential to complete team building but they can also be expensive. The advice must be to move modestly so as not to increase costs beyond what can be supported. If the situation is explained clearly to employees and there is definite action in the team-building programme, the organization can look to beneficial effects in costs, productivity and general performance. It has to be acknowledged, however, that there is no obvious and certain connection between a team-building programme and business success. Like anything else the company has to get it right.

Propaganda and manipulation

It should be obvious from the above that the type of communications being planned for in a human resource environment goes further than the mere passing of information from manager to manager. It should also be clear that HR, with its concentration on people, has no room for propaganda and manipulation. These words are taken to refer to covert attempts to change attitudes or deliberate attempts to mislead. It is not necessary always to communicate comprehensively but it is always essential to communicate truthfully. Nor is it acceptable to argue that no direct untruths have been told, if the whole truth has not been told either. If the communication is selective to such an extent that employees draw conclusions that with more information would be significantly different, then covert manipulation (more bluntly called lying) is taking place.

In terms of the tenor of communication, managers in an HR framework are aiming at the longer term. There will be occasions when the message received today is important. By and large, however, the objective will be to establish good, reliable and straightforward communications over an extended period. This is often a mistake that is made. In a natural desire to make an impact, strong colourful language, sharply divided into blacks and whites, is used. This is propaganda and will be seen as such by employees and consequently not believed. Trade unions and to a lesser extent some managers, frequently slip into this trap. Once a reputation has been gained for sharp practice it is most difficult to recover. In communication, 'honest, decent and true' are the watchwords. In HR terms the objective is to win the long-term battle for the commitment of employees. This is not done by achieving their support through trickery on a short-term basis.

Auditing employee relations in an HR environment

As with all aspects of management it is important to have some mechanism for assessing the performance of the employee relations and communications processes. This can be done by various types of attitude survey. (In addition of course the manager can under-take her or his own assessment by simply asking employees how effective they think the department is!)

It is not even necessary to be overawed by the thought of detailed enquiries. One example of the results from an employee survey is shown in Figure 8.3. Apart from the direct usefulness of informa-tion gained from such a survey, the results can be built into a manager's own performance targets. For example a manager who had achieved a 'satisfactory' rating from 25 per cent of employees could be given the objective of increasing this to 50 per cent in 12 months. In order to achieve such a change the manager would have to consider a catalogue of initiatives to develop communication, understanding, trust and so on. There are many organizations which have developed such practices and those undertaken by British Telecom are particularly challenging.

It is also possible to develop the attitude survey into a more information-seeking audit. Sid Jennings at Templeton College, Oxford has, with government funding, developed a very useful audit. The terms are often important and therefore such audits can variously be called 'industrial relations review', 'company com-munications investigations' and various other names. An example of the headings covered by the Jennings audit is shown in Figure 8.4. The type of questions that might be used are given in Figure 8.5.

Such audits are not exact but they provide a useful reference point and in the right hands can result in stimulating discussion. For example, one survey showed that managers from levels 2–5 in an organization believed that they took communications with employees seriously and were good at it, but their employees did not agree!

Question: With regard to the means by which employees are at present receiving information relevant to their jobs, how would you rate the importance of the following? (Please answer all sections)

	Extremely Important	Very Important	Quite Important	Not Important
1) Departmental managers	8	33	52	7
2) Personnel	4	9	38	49
3) The supervisor	15	43	31	11
4) The trade union	29	32	24	15
5) Notice boards	12	22	55	11
6) Internal publications and circulars	12	25	61	2
7) The grapevine	42	34	20	4

Question: To what extent do you agree with the following statement? 'Managers have adequate information to keep their employees well informed about the current situation in the Company as it affects the department.'

Agree	Tend to Agree	Tend to Disagree	Disagree
38	43	12	7

Question: To what extent do you agree with the following statement? 'In practice employees are kept well informed by management about the current situation within the Company as it affects their jobs.'

Agree	Tend to Agree	Tend to Disagree	Disagree
2	10	71	17

All numbers are percentages.

Source: Private company survey by S. Jennings of Templeton College, Oxford, 1986

Figure 8.3 Managers' Success in Communicating with their Teams: the Results of an Employee Survey

List of Sections in Questionnaire		
1 General		P1 Q1-Q2
2 The Introduction of Technological Change and Reorganization of Work		P2 Q3-Q11
3 The Application of Terms and Conditions of Employment		P5 Q12-Q31
4 Implementation of the Disciplinary Procedure		P10 Q32-Q45
5 Communication, Consultation and Participation Arrangements		P13 Q46-Q59
6 Dealing with Trade Unions		P18 Q60-Q78
7 Provision of Equal Opportunities		P22 Q79-Q91
8 Implementation of Health and Safety Provisions		P24 Q92-Q102
9 Summary		P29 Q103

Source: Private company survey by S. Jennings of Templeton College, Oxford, 1990 and J Bramham 1992

Figure 8.4   Oxford Employee Relations Audits

Employee opinion surveys

Many organizations find that an audit of the type referred to above would have greater value if it was continuously reviewed. For this reason, opinion surveys which have some tough questions and tough answers have become increasingly popular, particularly among organizations of significant size.

They have naturally some similarity to audits but their purpose has an altogether sharper focus in an HR environment. Since they are often undertaken by an outside consultant on behalf of a company, this has the added value of improving credibility with the

Q49

With regard to the means by which employees are at present receiving information relevant to their jobs, how would you rate the importance of the following?

		Extremely Important	Very Important	Quite Important	Not Important	
1	Departmental Managers	1	2	3	4	(32)
2	Personnel	1	2	3	4	(33)
3	The Supervisor	1	2	3	4	(34)
4	The Trade Union	1	2	3	4	(35)
5	Notice boards	1	2	3	4	(36)
6	Internal publications and circulars	1	2	3	4	(37)
7	The grapevine	1	2	3	4	(38)

Q50

To what extent do you agree with the following statement?

'In practice employees are kept well informed by management about the current situation within the Company as it affects their jobs.'

Agree	Tend to agree	Tend to disagree	Disagree	
1	2	3	4	(49)

Source: Private company survey by S. Jennings of Templeton College, Oxford, 1990 and J Bramham 1992

Figure 8.5   Oxford Employee Relations Audits Communication, Consultation and Participation Arrangements

employee. One further point is that, if the external supplier has enough clients, then the data can be presented to the company in a way which allows your own data to be compared to other organizations in similar circumstances. This facilitates a benchmarking of factors to ascertain where problems may exist and what action can usefully be taken.

Summary

Employee relations within a human resourcing framework is not the same as traditional industrial relations, though clearly where there are trade unions they will be a factor to consider. The purpose of a strategy for employee relations is to work towards the development of the committed employee. This means building teams which are based on mutual support and action within the company. The key motivator of the team is seen as the supervisor and the company should do all it can to emphasize and increase the status of that role. As part of the strategy of HR, communications are crucial. These should be two-way and based on communicating understanding not information, and should relate to matters of relevance to employees such as job performance, sales, profit and budget forecasts and so on. Finally, the measurement of employee views should be undertaken and maintained and standards for improvement established.

Chapter 9

Employee Relations and Trade Unions

Trade unions and HR

A key element in human resources is team-work, along with the tendency to concentrate on the work group. One effect of this, as discussed in Chapter 8, is that a great deal of effort will be expended on making employees understand what the company is about. This integration of belief would then result in the company's beliefs being aligned with those of the employee and vice versa. One further result of the HR approach which has already been referred to is that a company will seek to treat employees with respect and give them the conditions they would want for themselves within the constraint of the company's financial success.

This integration of the company and the employee puts trade unions in an interesting situation. Many companies have reflected the shift from personnel to HR management in the terms they use to describe their relations with trade unions. Some time ago 'labour relations' (with the suggestion that people were not involved!) gave way to the more respectable 'industrial relations'. But workers (at least in manual agreements) continued to exist and only staff and perhaps only senior staff were 'employees'. But now the process has moved on. As the previous chapter shows 'human resourcing', with its emphasis on direct contact between team-leader and employee, is set to replace forever the traditional shop-floor approaches. Under the old system, companies did not seem to employ people – they subcontracted them with the union's permission!

Whether these changes are real and motivated by a desire to treat people with dignity and integrity or masks for old-style short-term strategies aimed at maximum financial return, is a point to be

debated. But HR as it is espoused (but perhaps less widely practised) suggests a fulfilment of a basic trade union aim.

Trade unions have in the past sought to raise the importance of
the employee in the company. But if a company has come to
recognize the centrality of employees – then whither the trade
unions? (See particularly Armstrong 1987.)

Trade unionism for the 1990s

The decline in power of the trade union movement has been widely
written about. (Metcalf 1988, Smith 1989, Beaumont 1987.) The
TUC in Britain has seen its membership drop from 12.2 million
affiliated members in 1979 to 8.7 million in 1992. Including non-
TUC affiliates, union membership has declined from a peak of
nearly 13.5 million (some 52 per cent of the workforce) to around
10 million (42 per cent) in 1992. This is shown in Figure 9.1.

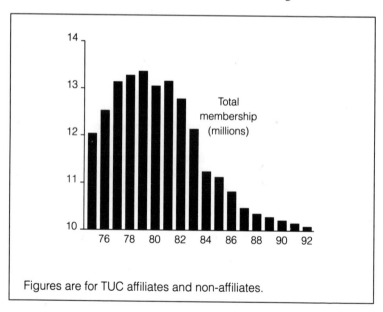

Figures are for TUC affiliates and non-affiliates.

Sources: Metcalf 1988, Smith 1989 and Leeds Metropolitan University
Seminar 1993.

Figure 9.1   Declining Trade Union Membership

In the USA, the American Federation of Labor/Congress of Industrial Organization has seen its membership fall from 20 million to 14 million over a similar period. Trade unions have sought to explain this fall by reference to the economic recession and the general reduction in people in work. It is true that the number of jobs lost in the 1980s, particularly in manufacturing, mirrored closely the fall in trade union membership generally. As Figure 9.1 shows, although membership declined rapidly between 1979 and 1982 this was against a backcloth of increasing unemployment. During this period the trade unions, supported by academic debate, argued therefore that their alleged decline was only the result of unemployment; when employment became buoyant membership would revert to former levels. However, what was being ignored was that new members were not being picked up among the then embryonic 'sunrise' industries which were using new, especially computer technologies. The failure to attract recruits in sufficient numbers in these areas may of course be temporary. Whether unions increase their influence in the new industries will depend both on their own efforts and on the effectiveness of company employee relations policies. Together the answers will enable employees to answer a recurrent question – are trade unions relevant to them.

Is HR incompatible with trade unionism?

Many companies and many trade unionists have begun to question the role of trade unionism in the modern corporation. In the UK in the 1960s and 1970s when union power was at its height, the movement failed to answer the question 'What are we here for?' The difficulties trade unions have experienced perhaps arise because the question posed is the wrong one. The question to ask is 'What *should* trade unions be here for?'

This latter question is crucial to trade union involvement in companies pursuing an HR strategy. Traditionally trade unions have concerned themselves with tactical day-to-day employment issues. This is alleged to have led to a neglect of wealth creation in favour of wealth distribution.

Professor D. Metcalf (1989) claims to have shown in a detailed London School of Economics study what many observers have always believed to be true – that union activity reduces employee productivity. In the UK between 1980 and 1985 a third of unionized workplaces suffered job losses while non-unionized workplaces achieved a corresponding increase. The study also confirmed that union-organized workplaces were inflexible, with demarcation problems occurring frequently.

The survey also shows that there is evidence that union activity raises pay – which naturally is an attractive proposition for union members. But the problem for the union leaders is that this concentration of effort on wealth *distribution* costs jobs where it is not supported by wealth *creation*.

The study generally provides a damning picture of the effect of unionism on pay, productivity, profits and jobs (although it is better on wealth distribution). The conclusion of such studies and of observation generally is that in many of their activities unions succeed in their short-term aims but at the expense of the long-term growth of the organization. Of course, as the TUC itself would claim, it is a debate a trade union cannot win. If wages are too high in unionized plants then trade unions are accused of pricing members out of their jobs. On the other hand if there is no differential then it is alleged that the trade union fulfils no useful function! These contradictions have to be faced by the HR-based organization culture. HR stresses long-term personal and corporate growth – can this co-exist with traditional trade unionism? If not can trade unions adapt to a new environment?

The collectivist culture

Traditional trade unionism has another related theme running through its practices. There is evidence of greater equality of pay in unionized organizations (Metcalf 1989). This reflects two forces. First, union members co-ordinate their actions and in so doing become a more homogeneous group when compared with non-unionists. Secondly and flowing from this, the union movement establishes its own goals which it then seeks to support by mobilizing the support of members. This is the collectivist culture which has been the central tenet of trade unionism since its beginnings. In 1903 Sidney Webb wrote that 'one trade union regulation stands out as practically universal, namely the insistence on payments according to the same definite standard and its application'. The dominance of such collectivist goals poses a considerable problem for an organization pursuing an HR strategy. The HR approach to managing employees seeks to integrate them with the corporate philosophy and to gain their 100 per cent wholehearted commitment to meeting the organization's aims. This will not rest easily with a trade union that is pursuing short-term goals that concentrate on wealth distribution rather than growth and creation and that seeks to achieve those ends by a collective trade union will. Unless the trade union can come to terms with the organization and its aims, they are likely to fall out.

The emphasis on collectivism and the short term has led to trade unions presenting themselves in an adversarial role. Of course, faced with corruption, abuse of employees, low wages and exploitation along with a resistant management, it is hardly surprising that an adversarial approach arose. It was equally necessary to develop in the trade unions a collectivist will, in order to create employee strength to counter a management that would give only what it had to.

The company pursuing an HR strategy will find an adversarial style and a collectivist approach not only unnecessary but irrelevant and in conflict with HR strategy. The HR company itself believes in highly paid and motivated employees. The HR company holds its employees in such high regard that exploitation would be inconceivable. This is not to say that the HR company has 'gone soft' and that profits have been replaced by altruism as a key business motive. As I have already explained, creativity, growth and service to the customer in a competitive market are achieved only by a committed workforce which in turn requires a constructive management approach to employee relations.

There is one further aspect of collectivism that will cause difficulty in an HR culture. The assumption that all employees doing the same basic job should receive the same pay is not acceptable to and HR-based organization. The HR approach will be to stress, identify and reward the achievement of the individual and the team. This will be particularly the case away from the routine end of office and factory work. At the supervisor level and upwards, the HR organization may well have a majority of its employees on some sort of merit-reward-performance scale. Again, the traditional trade union approach will not find this easy to live with.

The problem of flexibility

One further area can be considered. Flexibility is important to HR organizations. The emphasis on personal development and growth will result in employees moving to other work more frequently than might have been the case in the past. Again, this emphasis is not based only on altruism but also on good business sense. The organization can only be sure of one thing – constant change is the order of the day. It therefore follows that constant adaptation and change by employees will be necessary.

The traditional procedurally based approach to management–union collective bargaining will inhibit rapid adaptation to change. The HR approach will be to establish flexibility to such an extent that employees are limited only by their abilities and not by arbitrary distinctions based on 'craft' or 'office'. The question of flexibility is discussed in detail in Chapter 5, but at this stage its implication for trade unionism is important. One by-product of flexibility is that many of the short-term barriers to change within an organization no longer exist. Therefore the restrictive power of the trade union (particularly at the shop floor-shop steward level) is considerably reduced.

Employee communications

The importance of direct communication with employees is central to HR philosophy and objectives and without employee support the organization will not achieve its most ambitious aims. The problems and methods of communicating with employees are discussed in Chapter 8. For the trade union such changes create an uncomfortable dilemma. Many closed-shop organizations accept the role of the trade union in briefing employees and indeed go so far as to have virtually no management–employee contact. This approach is directly contrary to what is necessary to achieve an HR culture, where regular day-to-day discussion between and amongst teams about change, the future and achieving objectives is the order of the day.

The new realism

The trade unions are not without people of intelligence and vision who recognize the changes taking place. Management and politicians are not slow to characterize the union movement as an industrial dinosaur unable to keep pace with the developments of the modern organization. Such comments are based on huge myths. First, the 'old left' wish to characterize much of the current managerial approach and supporting 'anti-union' legislation as having disturbed the idyll of employers and employed co-operating in an age of harmony.

The second myth is that presented by the 'new right' as re-establishing a golden age of employer-led enterprises which existed before humanity and personal fulfilment were disturbed by the interventions of self-seeking and irrational trade unions!

Both conveniently forget their history. The right forget that trade unions arose during a period of unimaginable abuse of human dignity made marginally tolerable by relative economic progress; the left ignore the fact that the 'new right' was able to sustain its programme only following a period of undisciplined collectivism and the subjugation of legitimate individual or separate company interests.

Perhaps trade unions are showing signs of recognizing that the HR company does hold its employees in high regard and that exploitation is for many a thing of the past. But the trade unionist will with some justice argue that many of the modern views about people at work are a fulfilment of basic trade union beliefs and they can express some pleasure that management have at last caught on!

In the US and Europe flexibility and long-term strategically based pay and productivity deals have become more common. Demarcation lines and industrial action have considerably reduced as the adversarial approach to industrial relations is avoided.

The HR approach has led to organizations rethinking their view of trade unions and unions have responded with single-union and no-strike deals. At the same time unions are busy reorganizing themselves. By the early 1990s there will be a few very large unions covering whole industries in the US and the UK which will overcome many of the rivalries that have caused difficulties in the past.

In addition, trade unions are responding to employees' needs and wishes by the services they offer. The health-care, house-loan and general advice service is replacing the pursuit of a narrow sectional interest backed up by an adversarial approach and industrial action. In a quiet but significant move the huge UK General, Municipal and Boilermakers' Union (GMB) changed its slogan from 'Unity is Strength' to 'Working Together'. The phrase 'working together' is very much what the HR organization is looking for. There are signs that the union movement is rising to the challenge.

Dinosaurs v Filofax

The transition of trade unions from an adversarial collectivist approach to integration within an HR culture will not be without pain. The trade union movement will rightly be sceptical of the sudden conversion of some managers to a belief in the centrality of employees.

Diligence will be necessary and there remain battles to be won in the areas of safety, equal opportunities and Third World exploitation. In 1988 the pain expressed itself at Britain's TUC conference at Brighton with the expulsion of the EETPU (Electrical, Electronic, Telecommunications and Plumbing Union) from the TUC. Although presented as an argument about single-union, no-strike agreements entered into by the EETPU it was more a battle about membership poaching in sunrise industries.

Despite such problems the trade unions will strive to reverse the decline they have experienced throughout Western industry. New-style agreements will include those aspects which will fit easily in an HR strategy such as those shown in Figure 9.2.

All of these need not necessarily apply at the same time. There are single-union deals that do not have no-strike clauses and there are multi-union no-strike agreements (eg Iveco Ford and West Terry printers). Indeed it is sometimes forgotten that the forerunner to the GMB established a single-union deal with the Becton Gas Works in 1883 and in 1985 the Transport and General Workers' Union (TGWU – the largest UK union) agreed a single-union deal in a previously multi-union company (and not on a greenfield site) with Norsk Hydro.

In the USA the AFL-CIO has established a 'protected area' scheme which limits the incursion of other unions into areas where existing unions are dominant. At the same time the British TUC

Single union for a company or site
Single-status terms and conditions
No-strike clauses
Reliance on the arbitration process to solve disputes
Commitment to job flexibility
Emphasis on training and retraining
Problem-solving rather than adversarial approach
Participative management style
Emphasis on employee participation
Importance of employee commitment
Annually based pay, paid monthly
Annual hours and flexible hours

But such agreements depend on:

Positive, firm and fair management
Employees being treated with respect
Equal terms and conditions policies

Source: Bassett 1987

Figure 9.2   Features of New-Style Trade Union Agreements

Bridlington Rules are gradually being reinterpreted to accommodate the changes that are taking place. The trade unions are also
looking at ways of improving the position in existing multi-union
plants where conflict can result from competition among unions.
This might lead to single channel bargaining in many companies
where currently multi-unionism has led to chaos.

HR is essentially unitary in approach and there will be no place in
a company's HR strategy for those who threaten the continuity of
the organization by attacking its basic aims. It should also be
remembered that non-union companies are not a product of HR
strategies. Non-union companies (IBM, Hewlett Packard and many
others) existed long before the current HR debate began. At the
same time there are companies which have embraced trade unions
when they might have avoided doing so (Nissan UK in Sunderland).

In the final analysis the answer may lie with the trade unions
themselves. If they behave positively and proactively as a strategy

rather than a tactic, then managers will be in real trouble! It is up to the trade unions.

Conclusion and summary

The developments described above are important for the success of trade unions in the HR environment. The successful trade union of the future will be softer and more sympathetic to the variety and variability of employer and employee needs. It will be more friendly and welcoming to new recruits and more informal in its appearance. It will seek a membership that wishes to join and not be coerced by the closed shop or the contract. Finally, the unions will recognize that strikes are bad.

The trade union movement in rejecting the adversarial approach will also recognize that employee aspirations for personal fulfilment will reduce the importance of collectivism. Finally, the pressure for change and flexibility will result in more efforts being directed towards wealth creation than wealth distribution. With these developments a different but vibrant trade union movement will find itself able to come to terms with the modern corporation and HR concepts.

Chapter 10

Equal Opportunities –
A Freedom to Try

Planning for the effective use of human resources implies making full use of the intrinsic talents that people can bring to an organization. Therefore while training and employee development are of significant importance, to be effective these plans must be carried out against the background of an approach that draws on all the people available. In addition organizations will need to ensure that there is no unlawful or unfair discrimination. Employees are not stupid – a company that behaves badly to one employee will do the same to another, and one day it could be them. There is much organizational self-interest in equal opportunities planning.

From the point of view of self-interest this matter is crucial to business success. The demand for skills and variety in the future is likely to place organizations in a seller's market. Skills, particularly in science, technology and human relationship areas, are likely to be in short supply. Partly this arises because there is not a finite absolute level of skill required. Consider quality and customer service for example. There is simply no limit to the quality that can be built into a product or service; there is no limit to courtesy and service. It follows therefore that however much such factors improve, the 'best' will always be in short supply.

It is therefore important that the organization does not necessarily limit itself in the search for people of ability and quality. It follows that all groups within and outside the organization should be seen as providing its potential needs. Equal opportunities makes business sense. Indeed the proportion of married women working has increased markedly over the generations, as Figure 10.1 shows.

Married women 'in work' (UK)

1911 — 10%

1931 — 10%

1951 — 20%

1971 — 42%

1978 — 47.9%

1987 — 53.1%

1992 — 55.6%

Source: EOC Report 1988 and Social Trends 1994

Figure 10.1 Social Trends

It is often the case, of course, that the exigencies of business stimulate programmes which might otherwise seem altruistic. In the 1960s Germany established a system of *gastarbeiter* ('guest workers') that at the time seemed forward-thinking and responsible. Certainly the Turkish and other southern European and Asian workers who benefited seemed pleased with the arrangement.

In the US the surge of technology led to a growth of opportunities for many groups previously regarded as disadvantaged. Many US companies found the barriers were swept aside when the need to find a COBOL 9 data architecture expert was required!

A similar situation is about to occur in EC countries. Falling populations in Italy and Germany and a levelling off in France have created a need to get the best out of groups previously hardly given a second glance. The UK situation is equally interesting but perhaps more subtle. The overall population continues to increase, but at the same time government statistics show a decline in school leavers. There is therefore a business need to ensure that new supplies of talent and skills are sought to provide the people organizations need.

Legal pressures

Business need is without doubt the best and most effective motivator but companies must also ensure that they work correctly within the legislative framework. In the area of preventing discrimination, tighter legislative control can be expected. Most countries have a substantial legal framework of anti-discriminatory legislation aimed at preventing discrimination on the grounds of race, creed or sex. In addition there is growing support to end so-called 'age discrimination'. This latter is already a feature of US legislation. Along with business need therefore, the need to keep in line with statutory requirements will ensure that action is taken. It should be recognized however that anti-discrimination programmes motivated by statutory pressure are liable to be minimal in effect – just sufficient to keep within the law. It is only when there is some commitment to a programme because of business need that significant action is likely.

Altruism

In addition to business need human resourcing can lead to action based on altruism. Over a longer period altruism – action based on a regard for people – can be argued to be a foundation of business need. If organizational actions are motivated by a desire to treat people as people then the organization will reap the benefit. This approach may appear a touch too philosophical for some managers and what happens when there is conflict between the way the manager might wish to treat people and the needs of the organization? It is not likely that organizations will be managed on the basis of altruism in any complete sense. But a great deal of sympathetic and human treatment is possible. It is not only possible to treat people as people but also for this approach to be beneficial to the organization and its continuity.

Analysis of present practice

Of course the starting point in any programme is to establish the base. For this reason some sort of classification is essential. If

	BLACK				WHITE		
Period from .... to	Afro-Caribbean Origin	African Origin	Asian Origin	Other	European Origin (including UK)	Other	Total
Industrial employees							
Maintenance	(a) (b) (c)						
Production (according to grade)	(a) (b) (c)						
Despatch	(a) (b) (c)						
Supervisory	(a) (b) (c)						
TOTAL	(a) (b) (c)						

(a)   is number of applicants in the category
(b)   is number of interviewees in the category
(c)   is number of appointments in the category

Note: This form is used to produce an analysis of recruitment patterns, but the same principles apply to surveys of total numbers of employees, promotions, training and so on.

Source: EOC and CRE

Figure 10.2   Classification System Used in an Analysis of Recruitment Patterns

classification is not undertaken it is not possible to count and without counting the extent of discrimination, if any, cannot be determined. Classification can itself lead to offence and therefore the planning of the process will need to be handled with care. One

Factors	Maintenance Fitter	Company Nurse
Skill		
Experience in job	10	1
Training	5	7
Responsibility		
For money	0	0
For equipment & machinery	8	3
For safety	3	6
For work done by others	3	0
Effort		
Lifting requirement	4	2
Strength required	7	2
Sustained physical effort	5	1
Conditions		
Physical environment	6	0
Working position	6	0
Hazards	7	0
Total	64	22

(Each factor is scored on a scale from 1 to 10; for simplicity no weights have been applied)

Figure 10.3(a)   Examples of Biased Job Factors

classification system recommended by the UK Equal Opportunities Commission is illustrated in Figure 10.2.

Typical analyses will show salary or hierarchical position compared with grade divided between various groupings. These groupings could be divided according to race, sex, or creed.

It is important to analyse current employees to ensure that potential areas of discrimination are identified. These analyses can be enhanced by attempting to identify the more subtle forms of discrimination which can occur within *jobs*, such as the way they are set up and evaluated. Figure 10.3(a) gives an example of the discriminatory use of job factors in a job evaluation scheme. It is clear that the factors are heavily biased towards the typical male manual occupation at the expense of the nurse – more likely filled by a female employee. In this subtle and covert way male jobs are given more weight than female ones. This result is not inevitable. An attempt to reduce bias in the previous case is shown in Figure 10.3(b).

Factors	Maintenance Fitter	Company Nurse
Basic knowledge	6	8
Complexity of task	6	7
Training	5	7
Responsibility for people	3	8
Responsibility for materials & equipment	8	6
Mental effort	5	6
Visual attention	6	6
Physical activity	8	5
Working conditions	6	1
Total	53	54

(Each factor is scored on a scale from 1 to 10; for simplicity no weights have been applied)

Figure 10.3(b)   Example of Less-biased Job Factors

Targeting

In planning for the proper use of human resources there is little use in classifying, counting and analysing if no action results. As a result a growing number of companies are adopting some form of targeting as part of their equal opportunity programmes as a way of ensuring progress.

Targeting can bring open hostility about the envisaged changes to the surface. New methods to encourage disadvantaged groups to improve employment or developmental opportunities can lead to legitimate criticism. This would be particularly the case if targeting led to positive discrimination in recruitment, which is illegal in the UK, although not universally so in the US where quotas in employment are common. There must be caution in this area. Managers will have to pay particular attention to the legislative framework in what can be a fluid area both in terms of new acts or interpretation of existing law by the courts.

It is unlawful to require candidates for jobs to meet criteria which are more difficult for different racial groups or either sex to achieve, unless the criteria are specifically a requirement of the job. It is the establishment and maintenance of fair and justifiable selection criteria within a framework of targeting that can form the key focus of an equal treatment policy.

The kind of targets would refer to recruitment levels, promotion levels and training take-up separately by the appropriate classification. The targets would have to be set to be achieved over a period of time. In the example given in Figure 10.3 earlier, it would be fruitless to set a short-term target to recruit females into the highest grades because there are no females in the source categories from which promoted candidates are drawn.

In summary the target is the result of the organization's various policies, that will be expected to be achieved over a period of time. The targets are not quotas and must not lead to unlawful activity. This is not an easy dividing line and care and attention will be necessary to separate the preselection process from the point of selection itself. It is for example possible to encourage women to take up engineering, science or technology as a career. To this end expensive and extensive campaigns have been mounted. However, while this extra effort can be directed at women to encourage greater numbers to apply there must be no discrimination at the point of actual selection based on race, creed and sex.

In summary, targeting makes business sense if it results in a better use of talent available within the company, opens up new sources of external recruitment or simply projects the company as a fair employer. Companies who readily accept targeting in other areas of their business may find difficulty in explaining why targeting achievement of equal opportunities policies is not appropriate (EOC 1986).

Contract compliance

One area of interest is the growing use of contract compliance as a way of improving equal opportunities in employment. Contract compliance is simply a requirement that a company complies with established (and lawful) equal opportunities policies before a contract is awarded to that company.

The subject is reviewed in a useful book by the Fabian Society (Carr 1987). In particular US experience is drawn upon to suggest ways in which European governments might progress. Figure 10.4 shows an interesting analysis of the success of contract compliance.

	Comparison of increase in ethnic minority employment by government contractors and non-contractors in the US, 1974-80*	
Job category	Non Contractors % Increase	Contractors % Increase
Total	12	20
Officials/managers	31	57
Professionals	12	57
Technicians	7	44

*The same differences in increases were found for women.

Source: Carr 1987

Figure 10.4   Contract Compliance and Equality

Equal opportunities or individual freedom?

There is one final point that needs to be explored. The very term 'equal opportunities' is based on a misconception. People are not equal nor can they have equal opportunities. Native talents vary from person to person and it is an illusion to think otherwise.

Moreover the human resource manager spends a great deal of time discriminating between one employee and another. Differences between employees abound in terms of skills, attitudes, human relations, education and so on. People are not equal and therefore their opportunities for advancement or achievement of personal aims will differ markedly.

The key issue for human resourcing is that the respect for people requires that they are free to stay and use their skills and abilities in the way they want. Organizations cannot provide equal opportunities but they can provide open access to selection processes and ensure that discrimination between candidates is not based on unfair or unlawful factors.

Summary

Equal opportunities is important in companies. First, an organization will want to ensure that it meets any statutory provision. Secondly, it may wish to project an image as a good employer to demonstrate that it puts faith in its people both to attract and to retain employees and also as part of a customer-oriented strategy. Thirdly, the straightforward business need is to plan for human resources and therefore all skills and talent should be sought out. This latter point is perhaps the key justification behind many organizations' programmes. Finally, targeting is needed. For the future, contract compliance appears to have been a success in the US, and might be applied elsewhere.

Chapter 11

Motivation – Achieving Committed Employees

In 1813 there was a mass trial of 'Luddites' in York. The hand-loom weavers of Yorkshire and Lancashire went at night with hammers to smash any new power looms. They were denounced then and have been since as stupid and short-sighted enemies of sensible mechanization and progress; the term Luddite entered the English language as a term of reproach and abuse.

But perhaps from this historical perspective the Luddites can teach us something. Those home-based hand-loom weavers were paid very low rates and could have earned more in the factories. Had this deep-seated and foolish prejudice another strain? Is it possible that the home worker wished to retain that small amount of control over life that the factory could not offer? Industrial relations experience shows that those industries most troubled are those such as old-fashioned motor manufacturers where people have to adapt themselves to the relentless and unforgiving rhythm of the machine.

Perhaps the production-line worker and the hand-loom weaver long for that little mastery over their work that allowed them to be people and not cogs in a machine. It is not fashionable to say so but perhaps far too much of people's work gives them a deep sense of an underlying disappointment at the way their lives are going, so they clutch at any change as an excuse for belligerence. Perhaps what is wrong with our highly industrialized and technologically advanced society is that it asks too many people to accept secondary satisfactions in place of primary ones. Secondary satisfactions are desirable and delightful but if primary ones remain unfulfilled, there will remain a deep unease.

Work therefore has to give people nourishment. It is as simple as that. The theories of motivation described below can, in their efforts to illuminate the details of motivation, mask this first and most important concept. What are these theories of motivation and how are they relevant to HRM?

Incentive theories

Crudely, incentive theories are based on the very old and established principle of the carrot and the stick. The presumption is that reward and punishment are all that is necessary to guide performance and to increase or maintain levels of production. Much of the research concentrates on payment as both the carrot and the stick and there is a great deal of evidence to support the idea.

Incentive theories can apparently be applied with success in certain circumstances. Key aspects appear to be:

- The individual must be able to relate extra performance to extra reward.
- Therefore the type of work must be amenable to specific and clear measurement and control.
- The additional reward must be worth the additional effort.
- The individual must feel that the system is fair and support the incentive scheme.

From an HRM point of view, this is not a tempting prospect. The emphasis on mutuality and team-work, and the changing nature of work with its emphasis on quality and customer service, all militate against incentive theories being applied in the long-term HR-based company.

The satisfied worker

The basic theory of motivation starts interestingly enough with the question of satisfaction. The idea is that if an employee is satisfied then increased effort will be the result. Handy (1981 and 1985) recognizes that this is not easy to demonstrate, however. But satisfaction may affect retention (so satisfied people tend to stay) and morale. These in turn will have a positive effect on absenteeism and labour turnover, both important from an HR view point. In terms of what has been said above it is probable that 'satisfied' in this context refers to secondary satisfactions.

The fulfilled worker

What form then might primary satisfaction take? There are theories which derive from general assumptions about people and work. In a sense they are not new. Niccolo Macchiavelli was well aware of the need for fulfilment as were Aristotle and Shakespeare.

In management terms it was Abraham Maslow who expressed the ideas in a memorable way. His 'hierarchy of needs' expresses the view that basic needs are only motivators while they are unsatisfied. When the basic needs are satisfied they no longer exist and are therefore not a motivator. This was expressed even more attractively by Handy (1981 and 1985), as shown in Figure 11.1.

There is considerable common sense in this postulation. We are all aware of the distracting and pressing effect that hunger or a call of nature can have on our well-being and composure. It should be no surprise if the professor of philosophy with a starving family puts aside a search for wisdom in favour of a search for food.

Theory x and Theory y

Maslow's ideas have themselves been expressed in popular form. Douglas McGregor (1960) set out two sets of propositions that he suggested underpin assumptions about motivating people in organizations.

Theory x saw people as lazy and workshy. The average employee lacked ambition and wanted to be led and to undertake duties following clear direction; there was no wish for responsibility and change would always be resisted. This is not dissimilar to the suggestion that management is guided by the 'thinly disguised contempt' (TDC) approach – the contempt too many managers show towards employees.

There will be many managers for whom this view of people rings

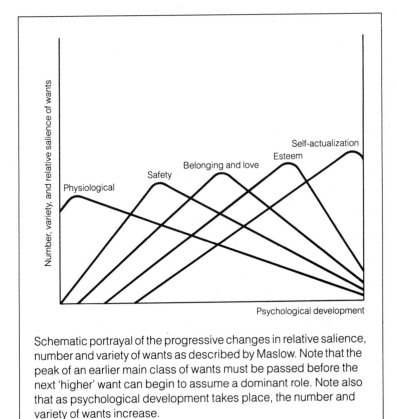

Schematic portrayal of the progressive changes in relative salience, number and variety of wants as described by Maslow. Note that the peak of an earlier main class of wants must be passed before the next 'higher' want can begin to assume a dominant role. Note also that as psychological development takes place, the number and variety of wants increase.

Source: Handy 1981

Figure 11.1   Handy's Representation of Maslow's Hierarchy of Needs

true. The manager was clearly the authority and had to battle for each increment of change achieved. Motivation consisted of incentives and a moulding of behaviour to the organization via rewards and punishment.

In *Theory y* can be seen much of the philosophy which is now reflected in HR management. In Theory y, people are seen as active and positive by nature. People are considered to have a desire for fulfilment at work and development and change are a natural vehicle for its achievement. In this context managers are leaders still but through facilitating and creating the environment in which creativity and adaptability can thrive. If people are resistant and destructive it is because of the way the organization behaves towards them. Whether destructive or creative, resistant or co-operative the organization reaps the people that are sown in its own attitudes to people. McGregor's full formulation is usefully summarized in Handy (1981, 1985).

Hygiene and motivating factors

This thread of satisfaction and fulfilment is also carried through into Herzberg's formulation (1966) but in a rather interesting way. Herzberg's two-factor theory distinguished between hygiene (or maintenance) factors and motivating factors. The argument was that a failure to meet hygiene factors would result in dissatisfaction but that meeting them in full would not result in satisfaction. Meeting *hygiene* factors would however create the necessary conditions for successful motivation through the *motivation factors*.

Hygiene factors would include company policy, pay, general conditions, interpersonal relations and so on. The motivating factors were the higher level satisfiers of the needs of people and included recognition, status, responsibility, advancement and work itself.

Context and contingency theory

This is very important for human resource management. It suggests that motivation is subtle in its effect and that, except in the generality, no model has been found that can meet the variety of situations the manager is likely to meet in practice. For the 1990s manager this could hardly be truer. Change, adaptation, creation and development will be the order of the day. The successful manager will be the one who can thrive on chaos, uncertainty and even ambiguity, or at least can handle them.

One result of this has been attempts (Fiedler 1974, Lawrence and Lorsch 1967) by social scientists to prepare formulations which attempt to aid understanding of the chaos. An important change is that referred to earlier – the recognition that the *context* of work is all-important – in a sense more important than the work itself. The manager would never be seen dead digging holes at work but will quite willingly grow successful dahlias at home. It is the context in which the work is done that is important.

The idea of context flows from the concept of contingency theory (Fiedler 1974). Put simply it is a view that employees' attitudes will depend on (be contingent upon) how the organization is seen. This framework will explain why an employee will accept new ideas in a company under threat but resist them in a successful company. It depends on whether the change is seen as being necessary for continuity.

The need for continuity

The recognition of context and contingency brings forward the concept of *continuity* as a driving force. Continuity is different from survival. This is a recognition of the intuitive and observed phenomenon, that people strive for survival in one circumstance – when their *continuity* is threatened.

The importance of continuity should not be underestimated. By and large people will maintain a degree of happiness and satisfaction if their continuity is assured. This concept also explains the different effect that the threat of job loss has in different environments. For example when full employment was the norm prior to 1970 the threat of job loss did not appear to motivate or control employees to any particular extent. This was not the perception in the 1980s. Competition threatened jobs in a significant way. During this period employees in the USA and Europe began to accept change and flexible employment policies. Such change, which lies at the core of a successful HR programme, would not have been tolerated some years earlier. Restrictive practices which in 1960 were seen as a way of ensuring continuity were now being seen as a threat to it. In terms of motivation the organization and its leader-managers have to persuade employees that continuity is preserved not by the retention of the *status quo* but by *adaptation and change*.

The task therefore in HRM is to gain the commitment of employees and improve their understanding of what the organization is about. This can be expressed as three things – customers, employees and quality. If the needs of those three are met the rest will follow naturally. In the longer term for example, profit comes not from a concentration on cost control or sales, but on customers and quality provided by committed employees.

HRM has to persuade managers that their controlling function is limited in its effect on customers and quality. This can be shown by exploring the contracts between employee and employer and understanding the assumptions on which the various types of contract are based.

Contracts at work

It is therefore important to have a clear idea of why people work. From the above the reasons can be divided into at least 4 categories:

Financial　　　　 – the money you pay to employees
Legal　　　　　　 – because they have a contract (for which they get paid)
Social　　　　　　 – for friendship and community
Psychological　　 – for personal achievement and fulfilment.

These can be represented as 'contracts', as shown in Figure 11.2. In any given employer-employee relationship, different aspects will assume greater importance. It is not important to decide that any one aspect is intrinsically more important than the others. The purpose of human resource planning is primarily business not moral concerns. Each has winning and losing aspects for an organization.

It is easy to visualize a relationship with a supplier which is predominantly aimed at the financial and legal aspects of work

Financial	– Wages paid
Legal	– Statutory framework
Social	– Supporting the workgroup
Psychological	– Supporting the individual

Figure 11.2　Types of Employment Contract

('You do that job to this standard and I pay you this amount'). Indeed this example points up the limitation of a financial/legal relationship – the emphasis is on task completion to a time at a set price. Is it possible though that a company wants something else from its employees?

Personnel people can readily accept that the nature of their contracts with an employer, while having an economic and legal perspective, has crucially important social and psychological perspectives as well. There is a good business reason why this should be so. The more you rely on pay and the law to sustain the contract with the employees, the less you will expect personal commitment from employees. Concentration on the task as the limit of the relationship will be less effective where the company expects an employee to create, adapt and perhaps redefine the task that has been set. It is precisely the need to create, adapt and change that brings about the centrality of employees in the organization and therefore puts in question the financial and legal perspective as the be-all and end-all of the company employee relationship. These ideas are a development from Gowler (1974).

Service and quality

Each aspect of the contract has defects and virtues. This is shown in Figure 11.3. Behaviour which stresses economic and legal aspects is best suited to routine, definable tasks but is less helpful for unique problem identification and problem solving. Where tasks stand alone (including highly specialized and technical tasks) and completion of the defined task is the key, then explicit instruction and control is suitable. Of course, this environment is of less value where the organization wants an emphasis on less easily defined criteria, or where work is interdependent with other tasks, or there is an emphasis on quality and customer service.

Take service as an example. We all know what courtesy is when we do or don't experience it, but it cannot easily be written down in its component forms (which is why specifications for employees refer to employees presenting a 'good image' and behaving with 'courtesy'). In the gas industry is the task laying on the service or installing the cooker, or is it to give a perception of quality and courteous service to back up, sustain and encourage gas sales? This

Taking instructions	Making choices
Financial and legal contract	Social and psychological contract

Emphasis on task completion	Emphasis on task quality
Stand-alone tasks	Interdependent tasks
Limited customer contact	Stress on customer focus

Figure 11.3 Assumptions About Work

problem of a company's 'product' and how to promote it underlies a great deal of the HR debate.

The perception of service, quality and interdependent task completion is also what underlies much of the personnel view about HR. HR recognizes the importance of social and psychological (even moral) pressures for convergence of employment conditions, of single status, the removal of antiquated class-based barriers to team-work (car-parks, multi-status restaurants, holiday and sick pay differentials), equal opportunities, career breaks, payment systems and the rest, including assistance for disadvantaged groups and employee-wide development and appraisal. It is based on the belief that the legal and financial contracts provide the background framework, but not the ultimate justification for the way an organization behaves towards its employees. In turn it is founded on a belief that how we behave towards employees crucially affects how they behave towards customers.

Of course, there are many that do not support this view or see in it an excuse for woolliness and lack of concern for business problems. If the choice was between employees and business objectives, I would sustain the business – no employee is better off if the business fails! But the caring and fair employer and the rigorous achievement of business objectives can coexist. Indeed looking at many large companies (eg Marks and Spencer, ICI, Nissan, Hewlett Packard and John Lewis), one can observe that the limits of achievement are only pressed by companies that work very hard towards achieving employee commitment through a clear understanding or what motivates employees at work.

Summary and conclusion

To achieve committed employees requires an understanding of what motivates people. There is no package of readily applicable solutions and the answers in any given organization will be affected by context and contingent upon a changing environment. The basic understanding that emerges is crucial to the philosophy of planning a new approach to managing human resources. The belief of HRM is that commitment among the workforce is the key and that is achieved by motivating people. In turn, while policies and procedures, pay and conditions are important, it is words such as trust, integrity and fulfilment that are crucial to the successful management of human resources. Given the right context and contingencies (it is difficult to gain trust if the company is closing), experience shows that extraordinary achievements are possible.

Chapter 12
Attendance

Attendance is a subject that for many organizations is a nightmare. The nightmare is usually expressed as problems of sickness or absenteeism. The traditional view of attendance is that some employees by their nature are shiftless and lazy and require strictly applied control mechanisms to get them to work. It follows that procedures such as clocking on, stopping pay for lateness, not paying for the first few days of absence and so on are regarded as essential elements in the battle to get people to work. The situation has occasionally become so severe that it led the chairman of a major British company to observe some years ago, 'We do not mind whether our workers come in on three, four or five days a week but we really would like to know which days they will be.'

Reflections of 'them' and 'us'

What this attitude, and the control mechanisms it leads people to adopt, betray is however a reflection of deep-seated attitudes to employees. 'Them' and 'us' is implicit in the absence control procedures companies apply. Clocking on and docking pay are particular approaches directed at manual employees and perhaps occasionally the lower-paid clerical worker. Those lower workers are also weekly paid on a per hour basis. This subtle mechanism is rooted in the view of such employees as itinerant and dispensable. No longer period of notice than a week is either necessary or deserved by such undeserving cases. Of course alongside this attitude there are terms and conditions which apply to such employees. Generally speaking they are excluded from the office employee terms and conditions

146

such as extended sick pay, longer holidays, welfare assistance and so on.

The argument goes that hourly-based manuals could not possibly be trusted to behave responsibly if they were given the conditions that apply to 'office' staff. The result is that crucial groups of employees, often at the very point of contact with an organization's customers, are treated in a cynical and untrusting manner. It is also important to reflect how conditions such as holidays and sickness are seen by many managers. The basic provision can be applied to everyone, and it is accepted that it will be abused by 'them'. However, for 'us' there can be extended privileges that befit the responsible way we will behave.

Of course if the privileges are extended to all employees the manager who doesn't trust manual employees is unlikely to be disappointed. Years of 'playing the game' by manual workers do not stop over night. Any extension of benefits is likely to be seen as a chance and advantage will be taken of it. The result is that employees abuse the new provisions and prove that the manager was right all along.

Bureaucratic control

The natural response to low attendance levels or bad timekeeping is the institution of control procedures. The clock provides a convenient tool and any employee who is late suffers the inevitable loss of pay. The same can happen with absenteeism or sickness. The problem is that such an approach develops an unintended attitude amongst the people it is directed at. While some will get to work on time, others will treat the loss of pay for loss of time as a fair swap. This is further refined into taking time off and losing pay over longer periods. (Indeed if the work is not done it may be carried into overtime.)

The response to this is to invoke the disciplinary procedure. The organization institutes some method of control such as an oral warning following three occasions of lateness, which is itself followed by written warnings threatening dismissal in the event of a repetition. Because many supervisors and more senior managers do not relish or believe in the process, it is passed to the personnel department. In the best tradition of action management computer printouts and exception reports are produced and letters written to be passed on to employees.

Such control procedures may stop the worst cases of abuses but in fact they do something more damaging – they institutionalize sickness and lateness. Employees learn which letters count and how much abuse the company will tolerate. Even worse the letter becomes a badge of courage earned in the course of duty (the duty being to 'abuse the system and not let them grind you down'). Indeed some organizations develop the absurdity to a fine art and negotiate attendance bonuses which reward people for not abusing the system! Of course no one can argue that an employee suffering a chronic or serious ailment should lose pay so those illnesses are excluded from the schedule disqualifying payment. Eventually the list becomes longer and looser until a further management 'buys out' the attendance bonus.

The cause of attendance problems

The reason for this apparent confusion is that the wrong problem is being addressed. Sickness and lateness are the symptoms and not the cause of low attendance levels. Human resource planning is based on a belief in employees. The organization believes that customers and quality objectives will be achieved only through committed employees. Those three corners of the triangle are the foundation of the organization's strength. From the human resource planning view point therefore it is commitment, not sickness or late buses, that determines attendance levels.

There are many examples of this point in practice. One originally highlighted by Neil Johnson is quoted in Bramham (1988) and showed the start days of sickness in an airline. The information demonstrated that for day workers Mondays are particularly bad days for sickness, as are Fridays. Gradually the week improves as few absences start on Tuesdays and Wednesdays. For seven-day shift workers Saturdays and Sundays are particularly bad days – Saturdays and Sundays are the days the shifts start and finish. In both cases Thursday is a day when sickness starts are avoided. It is not difficult to discover on which day these weekly-paid employees receive their cash pay-packets!

Similar and perhaps more worrying analyses make clear that

sickness levels of employees with a similar age distribution and identical occupations vary considerably. Why is it that sickness apparently strikes down the employees in one factory to a different extent from another?

It is also interesting to consider sickness duration to identify the true cause of the problem. It is true that the long-term illness will be noticeable and serious both for the organization and for the employee. In addition, for the smaller department, long-term illness will have a dramatic effect on overall absence levels and percentages. However, investigations have shown that long-term absence often accounts for only 20 per cent of total absence. The problem is usually the large number of days lost due to relatively short absences.

Indeed the effect is more serious than it may seem at first sight. This is because of the relative randomness of short absences and the destabilizing effect they are likely to have on production or service levels. Sixteen weeks' absence due to one employee with a broken leg is much easier to deal with than 32 employees having two or three days off each week over the 16-week period. Stability is an important consideration in production quality. It can appear that the cost of absence is the same because sickness levels are the same. However, the underlying causes and the effect on production and service standards will be significantly different. The direct financial consequences of attendance problems are only one factor and perhaps not the most important – stability can also be a consideration. Yet despite the evidence medical officers, personnel officers and managers continue to attack the symptoms and not the cause of attendance problems.

Commitment not sickness determines attendance levels

For an organization believing in people (customers and employees) and quality, the diagnosis, if not the cure, is straightforward. Absence levels or patterns of the type referred to above are a result of commitment problems in the organization. Certainly the separation of diagnosis and cure is an important one – inbuilt attitudes are not easily changed. Somehow the cycle of cynicism backed up by thinly disguised mutual contempt has to be broken. The 'greenfield' site will provide one opportunity, as will the takeover, the threatened bankruptcy and the like. What though of the organization that will continue to exist and is not likely to experience any cataclysm?

In human resourcing terms the transfer must be undertaken with careful planning. A simple harmonization of terms, benefits and conditions is more likely to lead to increased costs than to a surge in commitment and a reduction in absence levels.

The first point to make is that it is not possible to adopt an HR-based plan for attendance control but leave the rest of the organizational behaviour untouched. Absence control is an integral feature of team-work, team building, objective setting and performance reward that runs through the planning of a human resourcing strategy. The final effect of an HR strategy will depend on how completely it is applied, which itself relies heavily on the extent to which senior executives are committed to customers, quality and a belief in employees as the source of achieving excellence in those areas.

An HR plan for attendance

Any HR plan must start with the supervisor. He or she is the key to team-work and team building and teams are the antidote to failures of commitment. If the supervisor and the team have a good work-oriented relationship and employees are motivated then there will be no need for the day-to-day use of bureaucratic control procedures. Employees will see that non-attendance lets down other members of the team and the motivation to attend is greater.

The supervisor is responsible for motivating people to come to work. In practical terms this means a number of things. When employees ring in they should *contact the supervisor*, not as is the practice in many organizations, the payroll section or the time office, the gatekeeper or whoever. For both the supervisor and the employee it is important that personal (telephone if not face-to-face) contact is made.

On the return to work the employee must arrive early and report to the supervisor. The purpose of this is not to exercise force or fear but to lay down the principle that attendance is the supervisor's responsibility. It is for the supervisor to ask what the problem was and whether any assistance can be given.

It is also necessary to ensure that supervisors have the appropriate back-up and resources. They must maintain or at least have access to the employee's attendance record. The supervisor must be able to take action without reference to others. This must include stopping pay, suspending sick pay, issuing warnings and so on. Equally of course the supervisor must be able to justify the actions taken to others if required to do so. Responsibility cannot extend to arbitrary action. Along with this goes positive helpful action such as the provision of welfare counselling or of medical advice if there appears to be a recurring problem. People do get sick and early identification and treatment will probably help.

HR strategy applies to all employees in the company. It is therefore necessary that the principles described above are *universally applied*. It makes no sense to try and separate one group of employees for selective treatment and then expect universal commitment. This of course ties in with the discussion in Chapter 8 on so-called 'single status' or more properly 'commonly applied' terms and conditions. There is little moral and perhaps no business justification for having separate sick pay schemes and procedures applying to different groups of employees in the same organization.

It is possible to write these principles down. One organization's example is given in Figure 12.1. This policy and its procedures can be supported by trade union agreements and guidance notes for supervisors. Far more important than words, however, is the management style and approach adopted. The same words can sound and be applied quite differently depending on how the context is viewed. Neither is it necessary to be woolly and 'soft' on employees in order to be fair to them.

Withdrawal from work

Absence in HR terms recognizes that in addition to illness there is some other reason that affects people's wish to come to work. It is well known (eg Harper 1987) that absence levels vary between occupations. Not surprisingly managers have least absence, with office workers above supervisors and craftsmen above labourers in their attendance levels. Interestingly this is inversely related to pay because by and large the lower-skilled will lose more money through absence, either because they are not in a scheme or because

Emphasis on employee-supervisor contact

Supervisors to counsel employees on return to work

Records and patterns of attendance must be available to supervisors

Any attendance control procedures must apply to all employees

Figure 12.1   Principles of Attendance Control

they lose bonuses received only while working. This is a blow to those who would argue that sick pay increases absences.

The clear implication is that absence is more to do with commitment and satisfaction at work. This is not a new point and has been made many times before (Wickens 1988). The result of a negative feeling about work is the wish to avoid it if at all possible. In this way any excuse is taken to have time off. This has been called (Bramham 1988) 'withdrawal from work' and represents the subtle ways in which employees seek to disengage from their work problems.

Questions of control

It is curious that some of the most effective controls of absence come about as a result of a concern for product quality rather than a desire to reduce absence levels themselves. This must be right. If it is to be argued that the causes of absences are not solely ill-health but are rather complicated by questions of motivation, it follows that it is in that second area that real and durable improved attendance levels will be achieved.

It is true that the first phase of an absence reduction initiative usually requires efforts at direct control. This can include such action as attendance bonuses, reducing sick pay, limiting time off, or making people attend work who cannot do their prime job but can undertake other tasks. Iveco Ford have tackled the problem using a variety of methods (Arkin 1993). Working with trade unions, a new sick pay scheme was devised which provided payment from the first day of any absence but only if sickness levels across the plant were 3.5 per cent or less during the previous six months. It is obviously not difficult to move from this position to one where a certain amount of money is set aside for a sickness fund and if this becomes exhausted the employees and employers have to increase their contributions.

However, the limitations of such approaches will be recognized in an HR environment. Such controls, if not supported by an HR approach, will reduce absence but will also be transitory in their impact. If it is explicit, the idea of penalizing those who are off sick will not go down well with employees generally. At the end of the day, we must motivate employees so they want to work for the organization. The strongest control pressure is likely to be 'peer group pressure' – employees believing that they are letting their colleagues down by being off work. That, of course, depends on the creation of teams doing work they want to do – and this was the effect found in the Iveco study. (Arkin 1993)

A question of attitude

It has often been argued (Sandwich 1987) that an organization gets the attendance it expects and the absenteeism it expects. The attitude of managers and employees is therefore crucial. In turn the HR organization recognizes that the attitude of managers plays a significant part in forming the attitude of employees. In human resource planning the strategy has therefore to be aimed at getting attitudes right and reinforcing appropriate behaviour. The importance of attitude is emphasized by the role of the supervisor who in turn is crucial in the formation of the attitudes of the people who form the work team.

The standards of attendance expected must be understood and good attendance recognized. Employees must be aware that attention will be paid to any absence and that problems (including health care or action to prevent abuse) will be managed quickly and effectively.

One other important aspect of attitude formation is the supervisor or other manager's own behaviour. Personal example remains as ever one of the most effective ways of establishing the culture of an organization.

Summary

The focus in an HR organization should be positively on attendance rather than negatively on sickness or absenteeism. The causes of and responses to attendance problems are often a reflection of a 'them' and 'us' culture in the organization. Bureaucratic control alone is not a good way of controlling absence. The important point to recognize is that high absence is a symptom and not a cause of the company's problems. It is commitment not sickness that determines attendance levels. In dealing with absence the importance of an integrated approach to HR planning as a whole must be stressed. In terms of tactics the role of the supervisor is crucial, and he or she must have the power and resources to take the action that is needed. Finally absence should be seen as part of a failure to provide satisfying jobs, with the result that employees will tend to withdraw from work.

Chapter 13

Manpower Planning and HR – *Vive la Différence*

HR and manpower

There is a big difference between human resource planning and manpower planning. There are particularly important differences in terms of process and purpose. In HRP the manager is concerned with motivating people – a process in which costs, numbers, control and systems interact and play a part. In manpower planning the manager is concerned with the numerical elements of forecasting, supply–demand matching and control, in which people are a part. There are therefore important areas of overlap and interconnection but there is a fundamental difference in underlying approach.

It should also be said however that this view is not shared by all commentators. Some (eg Bennison and Casson 1984) would define manpower planning so widely that they would include virtually any area of planning or strategic processing in personnel management. More recently the position has been further changed and perhaps confused by the retitling that has taken place in much personnel literature. For example Thomason in the 1988 edition of *A Textbook of Human Resource Management* writes:

> Human resource planning (or manpower planning) may be defined as a process whereby courses of action are determined in advance and continually updated, with the aim of ensuring that:
>
> a) the organization's demand for labour to meet its projected needs is as accurately predicted as the

adoption of modern forecasting techniques allows and
b) the supply of labour to the enterprise is maintained by deliberate and systematic action to mobilize it in reasonable balance with these demands.

Thomason is arguing that HRP and manpower planning are the same thing.

There are those (Legge 1989/90) who have the suspicion that HRP will turn out to be the old wine of personnel management in new bottles. That is not the core theme of this text and would certainly disappoint the number of 'excellence' writers (Peters and Waterman 1982, Pettigrew 1986, Sparrow and Pettigrew 1988, Hendry 1987) who perceive new ways and new hope in the management of people. This chapter therefore will set out the essential differences between HRP and manpower planning while making the overlap clear.

Human resource management and the critical role of manpower planning

To facilitate the management of materials, money and people a whole range of disciplines of management have emerged: market planning, production management, financial control, business administration, human resource management and so on.

Manpower planning practitioners have recognized much self-indulgence in this personnel management and see a need for discipline, order, fact and information to influence personnel decision making. This is the role of manpower planning in personnel management. It is not another personnel discipline but an approach that adds a further dimension of fact and not fancy to the management of people at work.

What the surveys have suggested is that personnel people spend a great deal of their time on operational matters. There is a tendency to recruit today the employees they needed today; little or no thought is given to tomorrow's needs. (Indeed management knows so little about personnel requirements that it tends to recruit and train what was needed yesterday, for it has often not yet determined what today's requirements are, let alone tomorrow's.)

This emphasis on planning should not be taken as an attempt to divorce planning from operational activity. While there may be times when the manager is concerned more with one than the other, they should be different sides of the same coin and not separate coins.

It is important to stress, however, that manpower planning is not a lifeline that can be thrown to a company in distress, though it may be helpful to liken it to the practice of navigation, as has been referred to before (Bramham 1988).

> The good navigator uses scientific method in applying his knowledge and skills, within the limits of the equipment available, in order to establish first his position and then his best possible course and speed, with a view to arriving at a chosen destination by the most suitable route. From time to time during the voyage he will take fresh readings; calculate what action is necessary to compensate for hitherto unforeseen changes in wind, current and weather; and adjust his course accordingly. If the wind changes dramatically the navigator is not likely to abandon compass and sextant, go below and pray to God to get him to port. He is more likely to apply his knowledge and skills to a reassessment of his position and course as soon as this is practicable.

If you are only concerned with a trip round the boating lake, perhaps sophisticated methods of navigation are not required; but if you want to round Cape Horn in winter, good planning is essential.

This holds true for managing human resources. In a small family business the management might get by without planning; but most are concerned with organizations of extreme complexity and difficulty, striving for growth and survival. In this environment planning, rigorous analysis and control are the best hope the manager has to control events rather than be controlled by them.

It has often been argued that planning and forecasting is so difficult it is hardly worth the effort. It is, of course, a paradox that as the task becomes more difficult, so it becomes more necessary. It may be easier to take a compass reading on your local lake than in a force 10 gale but the first will be of no value, while success in the second may be vital for survival.

Of course the best-laid plans will go awry. The navigator may have to replot the route several times during the voyage but he does not conclude that navigation is not worthwhile but rather the opposite. Indeed it may be necessary in the face of some unforeseen problem to change route and reassess prospects but in using specialized equipment and techniques designed for the purpose, the craft is more likely to arrive at the chosen destination than if he simply lets the wind and currents take charge. The practice of management implies an ability to identify and select goals to achieve the objectives of the organization. If you are concerned with managing people there is no choice between planning and not planning. Decisions which affect the future (graduate recruitment, building new factories) are made whether or not planning takes place. The choice is whether to be systematic in making decisions about the future or whether to be swept along by events.

A specific HR contribution is to be wary of a tendency to rely too heavily on statistics. The search for precision may be laudable, but in respect of people it can be illusory. For some years, personnel managers have avoided involvement in planning because of its statistical content and to some extent they still do. It would be wrong to diminish the need for calculation where appropriate but it is possible to be involved in successful manpower planning even if you get your child's homework wrong! It should also be recognized that in HRP it is not the object of the process itself to have specific numerically expressed plans. This would be the business of manpower planning.

Spurs to HRP and manpower planning

It is interesting to contrast those matters which have been a spur to the growth of HRP with those that have led to manpower planning. Two key aspects leading to an interest in manpower planning have been technological change and manpower shortages.

Technological change in many occupations may result in the employment of fewer people but with greater skills. This leads to a consequent increase in the time needed for training (and costs, if inexperienced operators make mistakes). The result is that a manager must know what her or his requirements will be in advance of need so that she or he can ensure that the supply of people will be available. This leads to a need to forecast and to plan to meet that forecast.

In a similar way the shortage of manpower has been a continuing problem resulting partly from the points mentioned above. Curiously even during periods of high unemployment the phenomenon of a 'retreat from employment' has continued. Jobs which are considered dirty or where the hours or pay are unsocial have proved difficult to fill. In the managerial sphere there are signs of increasing reluctance to accept promotions which involve relocation. This is the 'trout farm syndrome' where managers are alleged to be eschewing promotion for private 'career development'. The result is that management cannot be sure that manpower of the required quantity and quality will be available – the supply and the need have to be thoroughly thought through and forecast in advance of the need.

The need for a linking of statistical with personnel practice led to the formation in 1970 of the Manpower Society which drew its membership substantially from operational research analysts and personnel managers. This small body remains remarkably influential at a national level and certainly stimulated the Institute of Personnel Management (which with the Operational Research Society co-sponsors the Manpower Society) into action of its own.

Finally while manpower planning can have a disturbingly dehumanized ring, personnel specialists often appeared to management as woolly thinkers, mere welfare workers not able to contribute to company profitability.

The emergence of human resourcing was spurred by more significant changes. Technology shortages were seen largely as technical changes resulting from the impact of demography or economic factors on the organization. In this sense manpower planning did not reflect a major attitudinal shift in managing people but was rather aimed at fine-tuning an existing system. This was not the position in respect of HRP. The emergence of the customer–quality focus led to the extinction of many companies which could not adapt. The collapsed industries in car manufacturing, shipbuilding, television design and manufacture, motorcycles, watches and the rest went under because they were trying to fine-tune their organizations whereas what they needed was a radically new approach. Although the effect has been much slower (because there were no market-imposed disciplines) on the producer-led organizations (state education and welfare are obvious examples) even there signs are emerging of a recognition of the importance of customers (and therefore quality and service). Human resourcing was the radical shift in approach – quality and service to customers can only come from people, not from systems.

National manpower planning

This area itself highlights an important difference between HRP and manpower planning. National manpower planning has two aspects. First there is the planning undertaken by government departments and other national bodies with a view to reaching decisions on national matters such as the allocation of resources to education.

Although this is an area where the company manager has an important interest it is not possible to have much influence and in any case any effect would normally be longer term – normally beyond the company manager's planning horizon. The concern is less with the planning itself and more with the need to identify the decisions being made and the effect of them on the organization.

Human resourcing strategy would, however, be more wary of a tendency to assume a necessity to forecast in detail. The search for exactitude except over the short term is likely to be fruitless and no more so than when dealing with national policies.

In an effort to begin the difficult task of formulating national policies on manpower the Government in 1974 established a Manpower Services Commission (MSC). This was a self-contained body separate from, though closely related to, government ministries such as the Department of Employment. The MSC was to be responsible for the management of government training and employment services throughout the UK.

While by no means the sole body concerned with manpower policies, the MSC had a central responsibility for achieving them sensibly. Its first major report, *Towards a Comprehensive Manpower Policy*, was published in 1976. One important example of the problems it faced is labour market intelligence. Without information on the labour market (the skills available, numbers of people, their mobility and so on), it is impossible to co-ordinate and correct the severe imbalances in labour supply that affect many industries

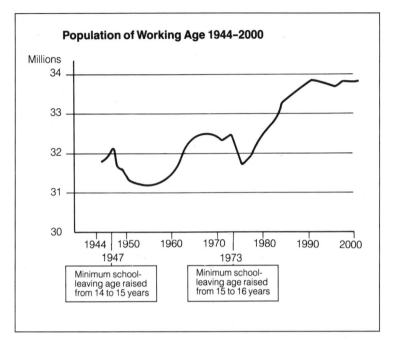

Population of Working Age 1944–2000

Figure 13.1   Growth of the UK Labour Force

and (it is claimed) would prevent advantage being taken of upturns in the general economy. However, the situation has not improved.

As a result of the problems encountered, national planning in the UK is dying quickly. The MSC has been wound up and training is to be handed to employers through Training and Enterprise Councils (TECs) and then, in a move similar to that in Germany, TECs may perhaps be amalgamated with Chambers of Commerce. The 'excellence' case would be that this is sensible because experience has shown that detailed national direction of economic policy is bound to fail.

There are areas where systematic manpower planning can help us understand the root of the problem and point to solutions. Figure 13.1 shows the growth of the UK labour force and future estimates. Between 1951 and 1976 2.15 million new jobs have been created. One reason why many households now have an unemployed breadwinner unable to find a job is that a highly significant social change has taken place. Figure 10.1 in Chapter 10 showed the number of women in employment over a long period to 1986. The importance of this is that it would have been socially unacceptable prior to the 1950s for women with young children to go out to work. Now there is even a trend for women to continue working immediately after childbirth. The result is that a very important social change has been a major contributor to the rise in unemployment. There is a tendency to discuss such matters only in economic terms, but the significance of these changes is that the solution to poor growth, poor productivity and unemployment might lie in social as much as economic areas of activity. Attitudes to work and overtime, and to who should work, as well as leisure and education, are as important as creating jobs by increased business activity. This recognition of the importance of 'whole people' is at the heart of human resource planning.

Education and training

This leads to the second area of national manpower planning I would like to consider. It has long been the view that it is not possible to match in any exact way the needs of industry and the supply of people from the educational system. This situation of separation, even of alienation, continues to exist, though new efforts at a rapprochement are in prospect (Confederation of British Industry 1988).

It is not difficult to argue that there is an absence rather than a failure of human resource planning in this area. Educational interests are accused of being inward-looking, and of regarding learning for its own sake as being the highest purpose in life. Meanwhile other aspects of life such as the job requirements of employers and the role of industry and commerce are seen as regrettable necessities and not really the concern of education.

While education should not restrict itself to producing people for specific jobs in industry and commerce, there seems to be no recognition of the possibility that life in the family, in the community and at work might be harmonized. Many people still behave as though there is an inherent conflict between work and education. The concept of human resources management would not embrace such an idea. Efforts to improve industry-education links (Confederation of British Industry 1988) suggest that major changes in attitude are taking place.

Manpower planning in the company

Within the company it is important to establish a conceptual framework for manpower planning that allows consideration of each part separately. Figure 13.2 sets out the framework for manpower planning. It envisages four main phases of investigating,

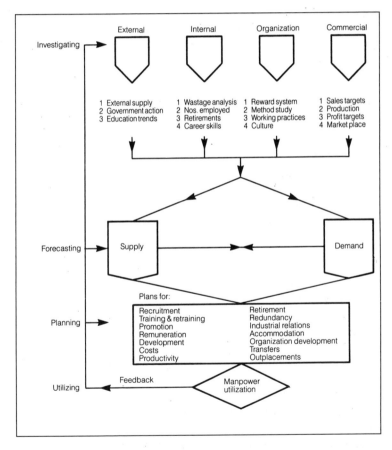

Figure 13.2   A Framework for Manpower Planning

which lead into forecasting. This can clearly be seen as part of the traditional activity of manpower planning.

This is less the case in the phase entitled 'planning'. Where the planning consists of routine matching of supply and demand such as through recruitment or provision of accommodation that would be properly regarded as manpower planning. Where, however, the concern is with culture management through organizational development or new approaches to career development and training, the images of human resources planning become clearer. In order to make the point and stress the difference, manpower planning belongs therefore more to the areas of control, the technical aspects of matching supply and demand and general numerical analysis. Planning of human resources deals more with the management of culture and of employees as individuals whose creativity, adaptability and enthusiasm are seen as essential elements in organizational continuity and growth.

In manpower and corporate planning circles people have been referred to as 'constraints' or 'obstacles' in the achievement of business plans. At the same time people are referred to as a cost. In human resource planning the difference is clear. People are assets not costs. People create and cause organizations to grow, they are not obstacles to growth. An organization that behaves as though people are a constraint should not be surprised to find that they are. It is a fair assumption to work on the basis that organizations get the response from employees they expect and perhaps deserve.

Forecasting

In the traditional areas of manpower planning activity, such as forecasting workload and manpower, further differences from human resource planning can be identified. The emphasis on the human rather than the technical aspects in human resource planning means that time series, forecasts and budgets have less direct concern. This does not diminish the importance of budgetary financial and numerical control, but it is not an essential first consideration of human resource management. Planning for human resourcing is more focused on culture, attitude and employee development, the argument being that when these are in place financial and technical control of numbers and costs naturally follows.

Employee development

The idea that careers can be managed does not come easily. The organization has to steer a careful course between direction on the part of a company and allowing the individual to mould his or her personal development as they see fit. That is not easy and one is reminded of the words of the manager who said 'I want my managers to act and manage like wild ducks – as long as they fly in formation'.

Effort has tended to concentrate on short-term aspects of management development such as 'Who will be the next vice president or finance director?' and 'If we recruit this person what training and development will be required to do the job well?' This is typically the work involved in succession planning – though it is hardly planning at all. Human resource planning adds a further dimension. Here tactical decisions are important but consideration must also be given to managers as individuals as well as a group. In this context one is concerned with questions such as whether there are sufficient engineers or accountants and so on. In terms of personnel activity such as recruitment and training the effect is that instead of asking *which* person should be recruited or should go on this course, the question is *what sort* of people should be recruited and *what type* of training they should be given – that is management in a human resource planning context.

Succession charts, appraisals and potential

Many companies rely heavily on what are called succession charts, an example of which is given in Bramham (1988). The purpose of these charts is to highlight short-term recruitment and training problems. The age of employees is indicated as well as who is nearing retirement; while immediate possible successors are emphasized. Employees' performances are also rated. Such charts can be a useful general guide for the short term to ensure that there is some provision for the future. At that point the chart should be destroyed or hidden until it is reviewed, say, a year later!

The problems inherent in the method are obvious. The appraisal of performance and potential is highly subjective. Managers classify differently, some being inclined to rate people more highly than others. The ineffectiveness of these charts for other than cursory use is shown by the fact that managers are never given poor ratings of performance but high ratings of potential and vice versa. Yet we all know that managers in the wrong job can perform well in other jobs.

There is also the problem of the Peter Principle (Peter 1970). This is an expression of the belief that because a person performs well in a job he or she will perform well in the boss's job if promoted. In this way managers continue to be promoted until they perform poorly; until they reach their level of incompetence. This process, Dr Peter says, is how 'clots find their slots'.

Career planning

The organization needs some way to look at career progression so that it is possible to ascertain at what rate employees progress, whether age problems will lead to promotion blockages or the overpromotion of inexperienced employees and so on.

One method is the career progression diagram. Figure 13.3(a) shows the percentage of employees at any given age in any managerial grouping and is an example of a career progression diagram. In the example above few managers in their late twenties have moved into middle management jobs, while by 35 more than half have done so. It also suggests that managers who are still in junior posts in their forties are likely to stay there.

This technique can be developed as shown in Figure 13.3(b). Here there is a noticeable kink in the chart and what can be diagnosed is that around age 40 a group of middle managers are not making the promotion they might expect – a promotion blockage. With this knowledge the company can respond with some remedial action (eg retirement or cross-division moves) if that is considered appropriate in view of other considerations.

More valuably the manager can build in certain assumptions about recruitment, training and wastage and see what the future charts will be like. They might show the situation is getting worse or perhaps that managers are being promoted younger with consequent problems of a lack of experience in the company.

On the other hand diagrams for different functions/divisions/companies can be prepared to assess whether promotion prospects

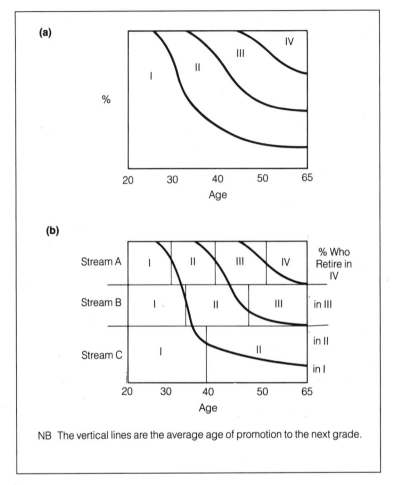

Figure 13.3   Career Progression Diagram

differ and an assessment made of the importance of this.

This approach is probably of more value in larger companies with a degree of hierarchy and it is probably more useful for considering groups of managers rather than individuals (though computer models simulating individual progression are available). The main advantage of using groups is that individual progression may well not follow a particular pattern, while trends are more likely to be discernible when groups of managers are considered.

At the level of technical control and forecasting these methods would correctly be regarded as part of manpower planning. However, where those aspects are closely linked with identifying and creating career paths and designed to release and harness employees' creative energy, then the links to human resource planning become clear.

Summary

It is not satisfactory to retitle manpower planning as human resource planning, though some commentators have done so. Human resource planning, with its emphasis on creativity, employee commitment and development is a distinct activity from manpower planning, where the emphasis is on forecasting, control and matching supply and demand. Although there are areas of overlap, particularly when planning careers and providing opportunities for employee development, it is preferable for the 'person' aspects of manpower planning to be absorbed within the wider framework of human resource planning and for manpower planning to remain as a separate activity concentrating on improving objectivity, numerical analysis and planning within personnel management generally.

Chapter 14

Power, Leadership and HR

Importance of power in HR

Without power no human endeavour can be successful. One can reflect what fine aspirations have remained unfulfilled for want of the power to carry them out. Yet though a knowledge of power processes is essential and despite 2,000 years of analysis, the subject remains as elusive as it is vital. This chapter discusses why power and politics are important in the HR environment and suggests a framework for the clearer understanding of their concepts.

There are two main reasons why power and politics are important to HR. First the rational model of management is discredited as the driving force in organizations. Managing by numbers has its limitations! Second, human resource managers can prescribe the best practice in the world but without the power to act, nothing will be implemented.

Therefore for the personnel function, the issue of power is central and in large organizations the need for power will increase. The skill to determine the content of personnel strategies is important but what matters is not what *should* be done but what in the context *can* be done. This aspect of power in management is too often ignored. HR is forcing managers to review outdated and dysfunctional concepts of an organization as stable and rational. Managers manage in an environment that is neither – fluidity and chaos are the thing now.

Peter Drucker (1955) noted that the emergence of managers as a distinct and powerful economic grouping occurred at a phenomenal rate. 'Rarely,' he says, 'has a new institution proved so indispensable so quickly'. He need not have been surprised. Management is an extension of well-tried and tested political formulations that have existed for centuries. Management in the corporation is a modern form of government. In both questions of power and political action (with small p's in respect of management) are central to decision processes. In the creative, ambiguous, entrepreneurial environment where managers search for an ill-defined excellence and 'thrive on chaos', it is inevitable that questions of power will arise. HR must ensure that such struggles have a positive not dysfunctional bias.

Failure to recognize power as a concept

Despite the importance of power, comparatively little is heard of it in textbooks. There are some established and widely read seminal texts on management running into hundreds of pages (eg Drucker 1955) that do not mention the subject, at least explicitly. 'Explicitly' is important because despite attempts to ignore it, consideration of power is so central to management that in truth it underpins much of what is described in different and quasi-rational terms.

An example of how this lack of recognition and understanding works to undermine creativity is in attitudes to leadership. Leadership is rightly seen as an important quality in business and the library shelves are full of attempts to plumb its depths. By and large their success has been transitory. This is because led by the rational model the attempt has been to discover those essential characteristics which are exemplified in leadership. But of course it does not exist as an absolute quality. It is essentially determined by the context and reflects the ability of a person to take others along a particular course of action. In other words it is an exercise in power. To HRM this realization is crucial. Without leadership at all levels in the organization, there will be insufficient drive for change, creativity, achievement of aims and so on. So considerations of power are central to an understanding of HRM.

A second example explains why companies hang on so desperately to outdated and even dysfunctional personnel practices. Divisions based on a representation of the British class system are retained by many companies. Curiously this is so even among those managers who would not openly support nineteenth-century British class culture with its stable and clear divisions and lack of mobility.

The company has the multi-status canteen, the managers in cut suits, the reserved car spaces and the rest. Such items should be recognized for what they are – symbols of a power based on authority, lineage and differentiation. Such approaches to power do not rest easily with a desire to build teams and to base organizational action on the efforts of committed and sharing employees.

Power rooted in its context

But an understanding of power would lead the manager to recognize that it is fluid and, as mentioned above, rooted in its context. Therefore, any power practice in HRM should only be retained if it serves business goals. The company that wishes to be hi-tech, growth-directed and customer-oriented will see that team-work and creativity, not clear bureaucratic structures and lines of authority, are necessary.

It follows that old power practices should be reviewed. The manager who is satisfied with the symbolic representations of a previous power will not find true team-work easy to work with. At best he or she will be in the way, and at worst disappointment at the fading past will lead to anti-organizational behaviour aimed at restricting growth, change and creativity.

Bureaucracy and closed systems

So in this chapter it will be argued that following the recognition of the sterility of the bureaucratic and rational school of thinking about how organizations work or could work better, attention moved in the late 1960s to the concept of culture and OD. This OD focus itself evolved from the failure of past human relations approaches to have any significant impact on managerial practice. There is now emerging, however, a recognition that concepts of power in organizations can not only embrace the strengths of the OD approach within its framework but can also explain and clarify much of what happens in any organization where relationships are complex and fluid, that is where ambiguity is common and where resources are scarce and competed for. In HR we are rightly searching for new ways to understand and interpret organizations and the relationships within them – a power and political perspective greatly enhances our ability to do so.

Some years ago it was possible to think of the organization in rational, ordered terms. Accepted systems and procedures regulated behaviour within the organization while the outside world provided a willing market to consume whatever goods or services were produced.

It was in this environment that personnel managers formed the view that organizations are like engines and that if any part failed, it could be examined, taken apart and rebuilt to make it function better. In this setting, organizations were seen as structured bureaucracies. Effective and smooth administration could be directly related to the strength of formal authority and the existence of clear written controls.

These ideas of organizations as rational systems have endured for a long time. Max Weber, an early exponent of bureaucratic theory of organizations, wrote his substantial texts between 1890 and 1910 (reprinted in Weber 1947). Meanwhile in terms of the study of work itself pioneers such as Taylor (1911) and the Gilbreths attempted to explain work in terms of its individual units that could be dismantled and reconstructed at will.

Despite changes, there is a great deal of evidence to suggest that these ways of interpreting organizations still linger in the corporate mind. For example, traditional work-study and piecework schemes remain popular even though the 1960s image has been tarnished.

The decline of the bureaucratic model

A number of major occurrences have threatened, if not overturned, this secure and stable view of managing the company. First the pace of technological change results in much that organizations produce becoming obsolete or irrelevant almost before the new product has settled down in the market.

A second factor driving much of HR is the rise of the customer. The pent-up demand of the 1930s and 1940s gradually dissipated as customers became more selective in terms of type and quality of services and goods.

After the Second World War, up until the late 1960s, companies became used to 'easy street' as demand for any goods was so great that customers would take anything they could get. This is no longer the case as was discussed more fully in Chapter 2.

Although many commentators would lay great stress on economic consequences, it is perhaps less certain whether economic changes are the cause or the result of other more fundamental changes. Perhaps the economic shocks related to the oil price rises in the 1970s exacerbated but did not create the fundamental problems that organizations now face. This view is supported by the effect of such changes in various countries. Japan for example suffered worse than most from an increase in costs, but nevertheless responded successfully.

The search for an adaptive organization

In this environment of rapid change organizations with fixed control systems and bureaucracies could not adapt to the changing needs of the market place. The organization that survives is the one that is creative and adaptive – but creativity and fixed bureaucratic control are not easy bedfellows and therefore traditional control systems are under siege.

It is a recognition that more flexible and adaptive ways of viewing organizations are needed that has led to the increasing enthusiasm for OD and culture management, in other words the understanding of the organization's value systems and how they emerge and change. This attention to OD (which itself has been growing in popularity for some 20 years) is part of the wider conceptual framework of HR, of which power concepts are a part.

However, despite its importance, until recent years discussions of organizations in power terms has been oblique. The importance of power and politics as it is currently understood is that first, it allows a framework to embrace different organizations in different states of development. Secondly, and perhaps most importantly, in an environment where creativity and adaptation are at a premium and formal controls are less important, political activity will increase. This is because creativity is intended to lead to the emergence of a variety of new directions for the organization and its products, but it also leads to uncertainty. But inevitably finite resources mean that those ideas must compete for attention. Without the formal control systems designed to distribute resources,

political activity is essential as the means by which decisions are made.

Uncertainty and politics and personnel

Power and politics are therefore enormously important for the personnel manager. It is worth restating the perhaps obvious point that the personnel role, because of its direct involvement with people, has always been subject to more ambiguity and uncertainty than many other managerial roles. The accountant has a better chance of formulating agreed conventions of handling and processing money than the personnel manager has in formulating a personnel policy. The fact that the personnel manager focuses on a resource that has quite literally a mind of its own has a fundamental effect on the nature of the job. This problem has been commonly seen in the industrial relations role of the personnel manager, where political activity of a highly destructive nature can prevail.

Apart from the personnel manager's job itself, which can by its nature lead to a greater involvement in power and politics, there is a second reason why personnel managers should involve themselves in such questions. In power and politics and all that they entail, we are probing the centre of the organization – its very being. If the personnel manager can contribute to and even dominate those areas, then her or his status (and of course power!) will be enormously enhanced. It is of course a matter of choice whether such power is used negatively (say for personal aggrandizement alone) or positively to benefit the organization.

Finally, the personnel manager is ideally suited to the role because the focus on employees and their relations with the company and the cross-functional involvement of personnel result in the personnel manager having a clearer understanding of the organization and its employees, and how they both work.

What are 'power' and 'politics'

Discussion of power is both old and new. The earliest philosophers pondered its intricacies, while modern social scientists have sought to classify its key aspects. One writer has clearly and explicitly set out a code of political practice. Niccolo Macchiavelli's stark conclusions remain the best source of practical advice for the modern 'prince' (ie managing director!) on how to gain and retain power and use it effectively.

First power can be thought of as the ability to get a person or organization to do something that would otherwise not have been done. Politics is simply what occurs when power and who exercises it is in dispute.

What conclusions have modern writers drawn about power and politics and how might these help the personnel manager? General classifications of power are common throughout the literature. For this purpose I shall use Galbraith's (1984) argument (though not always his terms). Power can be seen as having three primary instruments:

> fear of punishment ('condign power')
> hope of reward ('compensatory power')
> commitment and belief ('conditioned power')

(the terms in brackets are Galbraith's).

Punishment or reward

Terms such as 'punishment and reward', 'carrot and stick' are self-explanatory. The importance of setting them out is to highlight that often the personnel manager is dealing with a management orthodoxy that sees only punishment (the stick) or perhaps reward (the carrot) as the alternative strategies. HR recognizes the limitations of the carrot and the stick as the sole instruments of power.

The stick (punishment), while effective in gaining short-term obedience, is essentially restrictive. Wrong (1979) has argued that 'force is more effective at preventing or restricting employees from acting than in causing them to act in a certain way'. Of course at the heart of the organization's search for creativity, adaptiveness and customer service is a need for employees to take the initiative in their jobs. In this environment the stick is a poor medium through which to exercise management control.

Rewards, in the traditional view of management, are what employment is all about. The HR approach recognizes the importance of reward and a new approach to reward management is emerging as discussed in Chapter 7. While the effectiveness of good rewards cannot be denied as a way of gaining control of employees, again there are severe limitations. The most obvious problem is that reliance on rewards risks a market-place auction for employees. At best wage costs escalate and at worst the organization loses its best people to other organizations willing to bid more at a particular time. This essentially short-term approach is hardly likely to be attractive to either employees or the company.

How then is power in respect of employees to be exercised and achieved? The best hope is of course to *convince* employees that the organization's aims are the same as the employee's and to generate within the employee that elusive but invaluable desire to create and find new solutions, new products and so on. This is power exercised through *mutual commitment and belief*. This is what the HR company is looking for – people who want to work for this company and in this way. This is also what people are looking for – a company which places emphasis on believing in the integrity of people.

The HR manager has first to convince fellow managers that there is a problem. For example, many line managers conclude that with recession, competition and changes to employment law the employees and their trade unions are in no position to deflect the power exercised over them by their employer through the carrot and the stick. While this may be true in the short term, it might change in the future with employees and trade unions gaining the upper hand, and it is a poor strategy to rely for employee support on their weakness and poor morale.

An understanding of power and politics by the HR manager will enable an argument to be put forward that shows that power relying substantially on threat and reward will work in the employer's favour only when circumstances are favourable to the company. That same basis of power (threat and reward) can equally be used by trade unions and employees against employers when the pendulum swings to make circumstances favourable to collective employee action through trade unions. The HR manager should be taking the initiative in changing company culture to strive for true employee commitment – one of the key objectives of HRM.

In a sense this is nothing new. Personnel managers have always argued for consultation and employee involvement. What is crucially different in viewing organizations from the perspective of power and politics is that participation is seen not as altruism on the firm's part but as an integral feature of the search for employee support in developing and sustaining the organization. In this way there is a mutual exercise of power amongst employers and employees with each influencing the other and causing them to change.

The sources of power

If threat, reward and punishment are the forms in which power exists, how are they expressed? Galbraith (1984) and others (eg Pfeffer 1981) identify three main sources of power, as shown in Figure 14.1. These are financial or material resources, organization and personality (or leadership). It is important for the HR manager to understand these sources of power for in doing so it will be possible to differentiate those that exercise power from those that are subject to it.

Resources
expressed through financial, material and symbolic aspects

Organization
expressed through employee's position in hierarchy, committees etc

Personality
expressed through influence, persuasion (written/verbal), moral certainty, an expression of leadership

---

Figure 14.1   Sources of Power

Resources

Resources (financial and material) and personal wealth provide an aspect of authority and purpose that invites, indeed commands, respect. Through the control of resources (or less frequently these days in organizations, the possession of personal wealth) the personnel manager (or indeed any manager) is able to purchase submission. So the control of salary awards, promotions, development opportunities, trade union negotiations – or simply signing expenses – all provide the manager with opportunities for control.

Organization

But that is not the whole answer. We are all aware of managers who appear to have great status, large numbers of employees and access to huge resources, yet their ability to determine courses of action in the company is limited. Conversely there are junior managers without the formal trappings who get things done and assume great power in the organization.

How is this achieved? The phrase 'get things done' is the clue. It is a question of organization. It has been argued (Handy 1985, Galbraith 1984, Pfeffer 1981, Jay 1987) that organization as a source of power is the emerging, and perhaps dominating, form of power in modern society. Organized groups achieve access to power by threat, reward and belief in their ability to gather resources and utilize them effectively. The key is to recognize the methods by which people of similar values, interests or perceptions come together and exercise power over others.

Personality or leadership

Personality is another source of power but rarely recognized as such. The word personality is a summary of those aspects of mind, speech, moral certainty, personal traits and so on that give a person access to the instruments of power (threat, reward, belief).

The literature (eg Galbraith 1984) contains an assumption that personality as an expression of power is less important than it was. The suggestion is that it is now being subverted by organization as a source of power. It is easy to understand why this conclusion is drawn. The chief executive may *think* he or she is powerful, but will find out just how powerful he or she *really* is (ie how powerful is his or her personality) the day following retirement! It then becomes clear how important organization was to everything the person had become. The 'captain of industry' was flattered to consider that he or she possessed great power under his or her direction. In fact the power was a function of the organization and the person was its practical expression. However, it is right to be uneasy with the conclusion that personality is not important to organizations. Are we all organization people now?

Power, personality and leadership

In the introduction to this book I referred to power and leadership. Leadership is the collective word that describes all those attributes which lead a person to persuade, cajole, influence or force others to a particular course of action. In other words leadership is an exercise in power. In the terms discussed above power expressed through personality can also be described as leadership.

The power and political perspective permits an understanding of leadership that caused earlier attempts at illumination to flounder. Leadership is not a question of separate pieces of a person's behaviour or make-up that in the right proportions happen to result in a 'leader' (Bennis 1959). Leadership is the ability to exercise power using personality. Like all power processes it is dependent upon the context in which it operates. So the environment or the culture will affect what is acceptable leadership behaviour. There are no absolute qualities of leadership that can be identified and packaged. Leadership is flexible and fluid like power.

This is important to the HR manager. The natural and correct concern with developing leadership in companies has been hampered because it was not explicitly recognized for what it was – namely a source of power to control and mould employees' behaviour and of course to respond in turn to employees' needs. The reason why the search for leadership qualities has failed and will fail is because necessary leadership qualities as a source of power can only be interpreted in the context of the prevailing political situation – the context. As the political climate changes so will the type of leadership required.

The HR manager needs to think hard about leadership. The various searchers for excellence (eg Peters and Waterman 1982) realized that creativity and adaptability, 'radical decentralization' and 'turned-on champions' were required. It has been argued that many organizations have so hedged themselves in with controls (of expenditure, recruitment, ordering of supplies, training and the rest) that change is virtually impossible – sterility rules. Of course Peters's 'turned-on champions' are ordinary people who he is pleading should be allowed to exercise power through radical decentralization, through their adaptability and creativity, through their course of action, through getting the best out of people and getting ideas to come forward – to exercise leadership.

Tactical options for using power

It should first be remembered that in human resourcing managers are dealing with people who have, like themselves, hopes, fears, ambitions, rivalries, jealousies, affections, concerns, integrity etc. All these factors have to be dealt with in the organization. It follows that the negative aspects should be ignored in a natural desire to accentuate the positive. Managers have to deal with people as they are not as the company wishes they would be. The various options are discussed in some detail in a variety of texts (Jay 1987 and Wrong 1979 are particularly recommended).

Some important clues to understanding power are given in Figure 14.2. It is hoped that the manager will see patterns of behaviour that represent much of what takes place in everyday business life at all levels. Power is exercised at the shop-floor as much as at the boardroom level, although it is the high personal drama of the boardroom that naturally exercises the interest of the media and the film-maker.

Politics and political conflict

Politics as a subject for study has a long but mostly negative history. The problem is that unlike other forms of management debate or management activity we cannot conceal that in dealing with the world as it is (rather that as we should wish it to be) the manager may well find action being taken that all would prefer to be avoided.

Therefore politics frequently repels. Kotter (1979) found that by and large people associated such words as 'repugnant', 'unfair', 'dishonest' and 'manipulative' with political activity. Partly this

Tactics of Power

Preparing the ground
Building coalitions – countervailing power
Understanding information as power
Understanding interdependence in the Corporation
Importance of symbolism
The power that comes from inevitability and creditability
Securing the escape – for you and them
Understanding legitimization of management actions

Spotting the Successful Manager

Awareness of power
Knows and uses power methods available
Takes calculated power risks
Deliberate use of power tactics and strategies
Gathers company resources needed to exercise power
Shrewd assessment of the key career jobs

Machiavelli's Advice

Pamper or remove people, especially opponents
Don't avoid the necessary conflict, but choose the moment
Innovations make enemies and a few good friends
Confer benefits gradually
Dispense pain quickly
Act before you are forced to do so
Let weak opponents escape
Never gloat over a victory
Judge a person by the friends he has

Figure 14.2   Training Managers in Understanding Power

negative feeling about politics stems from an understandable but wrong analysis. As the saying goes, 'Successful people are self made, while failures are the victims of their environment.' This is the attitude surrounding politics. Successful candidates for promotion pride themselves on their ambition, skill and the hard work which resulted in their achievement. The failed candidate seeks to blame 'office politics'. If it's good I did it – if it's bad 'they' (ie the office politicians) unfairly ganged up on me.

The truth is that politics plays its part equally in the good and the bad. There is nothing essentially cynical or evil about politics. But we present the good as something different. Questions of power and politics run through all management behaviour and are particularly relevant to the HR manager. The first priority for HR is therefore to recognize the importance of the political activity, both good and bad, which runs throughout any action within the organization.

Understanding power – training managers

One important aspect of power and politics that the HR manager must deal with is that 'radical decentralization' and giving 'turned-on champions' their head will result in increased political, if positive and progressive, activity. This is because political activity intensifies when the exercise of power is disputed. In the strictly and formally controlled environment typical of many companies there are relatively fewer disputes at junior level. In these circumstances only at the highest level is there a dispute about power and therefore political activity occurs at that level. This is one reason why executives appear more political than the rest of us. However, with decentralization and the freedom to make decisions at lower levels in the organization political activity will increase there also. The question for HR is whether our supervisors and junior managers are trained to handle this increasingly complex environment.

Certainly there is little explicit reference to questions of power in management training courses. In addition it is worth noting how few courses exist on the subject. Even the IPM, which includes it in its courses, does so as a piece of add-on social science rather than as a key driving force behind all corporate behaviour.

What issues might be trained for?

First a discussion of power and politics would make it possible in training to challenge people's assumptions about organizations. Despite a widespread acceptance in the personnel function of the importance of human aspects in management, there remains among line management an extraordinary faith in those carrots and sticks, in formal control systems, and a general belief that rational procedures and structural changes can solve everything.

In Search of Excellence and *The Winning Streak* make clear what distinguishes the successful company. The personnel function needs to ponder the message of such books long and hard.

Training can go further. Wrong (1979) has classified the operation of power through various tactical options and an amalgamation of those is shown in Figure 14.2. Training can explore the extent to which authority can be relied on as an exercise in power. Authority refers to the power conferred on a manager by virtue of holding a job. As a basis for management the use of authority is not always likely to result in committed employees who create and adapt in their jobs. An important concern in HRM is legitimation – is something seen as fair and reasonable? This applies especially to authority. Legitimate authority relies heavily on two instruments of power – threat and reward. We must train managers how to grasp the third – producing employees with commitment and belief. This is the purpose of HRM. The HR function is to ensure that the opportunities in HR are planned for.

Another aspect of power is the ability to coerce employees to behave in a particular way. Coercion is a necessary tactic but a manager needs to understand that such methods of managing are better at restricting behaviour than positively leading to the type of behaviour required. Adaptability, growth and commitment are less likely to emerge in an organization where restriction and controls are at a premium.

Attitudes of employees

A further key area for training is to explore the problems for managers of a workforce with changing attributes and aspirations. There is evidence that employees will not accept arbitrary authority. In any event organizations in rapid technical change require adaptive and creative employees. Further the technical detail of jobs and customer contact increasingly calls for employees who will take initiatives and respond positively. This has enormous impact for the way organizations are managed and the way control systems operate.

Dan Gowler in his studies on supervisors (1974) has remarked that many of our traditional problems with first- and second-line supervisors can be traced back to the fact that we make them responsible for our first asset (our people), we shower them with our second most important asset (costly materials and equipment), but swamp them with controls that stop them taking the team out for a Christmas drink.

Symbolism

This latter aspect is crucial. People respond less to rational systems and more to the 'feel' of things. For this reason symbolism is emerging as a key area in any understanding and application of HRM. People can accept the irritants of life and the things that go wrong (in a sense the bigger the disaster the better is likely to be the committed employee's response!), as long as the basic thrust is seen as legitimate and consistent. Incidentally the fact that we are, thankfully, incredibly forgiving of each others' foibles is why the human relations school failed to offer any significant breakthrough in managing people. Symbolism is extraordinarily important in exercising power in any walk of life and no less in management.

Legitimacy and trust

A natural concern about power is that it could be misused – that we will get more office politics and fewer co-operative ventures. This is perhaps to the way some people feel about nuclear power – perhaps it would have been better left uninvented! The problem is that power and its use (politics) exists and the successful HR-based organization will seek to concentrate on its strengths and minimize its dysfunctional aspects. For this reason legitimacy can be shown to be crucial in how power is exercised. Going through the motions of consultation with embittered trade unions may be tiresome but it is an integral part of a process which over time legitimizes management action. However ritualistic a manager's action may be, it needs to be understood that to short-circuit expected behaviour and channels will mean that any resultant action is seen as illegitimate.

Related to legitimacy are problems of trust. As policy action takes place in an uncertain environment (ie there is a contest for power) the managers involved have to abide by certain rules. The particular ethics and standards of behaviour are important but they should also be better understood and operated.

The answers therefore to those who query whether power should be openly discussed and trained for is that managers have no choice. In the HR-based company the emphasis on human and therefore inevitably ambiguous qualities makes this more important. It is a recognition that commitment is central to HR organizations. It is then the recognition that commitment is not a rational mechanical response, but one based on mutuality, trust and integrity. Finally the achievement of the commitment of employees is the result of a power relationship which does not have to be cynical or exploitative to be effective.

Summary

Power has been shown as a key concept in the management of organizations. Organizations exist in a fluid and challenging world where what *can* be done is often more important than what *should* be done. What can be done rests on the power available. Power has three primary instruments by which it is exercised:

Fear of punishment
Hope of reward
Commitment and belief

Sources of power are rooted in:

Economic or material resources
Organizational power
Personality or leadership

Of the instruments, commitment is central to HR and substantially replaces a reliance on punishment and reward. Of the sources of power, personality or leadership is seen as a key to successful HR and again is a neglected area of activity for much organizational behaviour.

Chapter 15

The Personnel Function, HR and the Future

Images

Karen Legge with D. Gowler wrote a paper entitled 'Images' (Gowler and Legge 1986). Its basic thrust was to question what executives said about their employees and whether that was reflected in the company report or in its behaviour generally. It was pointed out that chairmen's statements are often couched in the language of polite thanks with minimal variations from year to year. How employees are seen and how the company behaves towards them is crucial to HR. There is a natural desire for the company to want to portray itself as well run and humane. Is the reference to employees as assets rather than costs or liabilities deeper than that? Gowler and Legge (1986) are not sure that there is anything humane in the approach, suspecting that the company's family image is useful because it blurs the conflicts that exist within the structure of an organization between those stakeholders who seek a return on investment and those who seek continuity in the form of a job, fulfilment and financial resources.

Does HR exist?

This itself leads to the issue of the extent to which human resourcing is simply another name for personnel management. There was evidence that this was the case. The example of the terms manpower planning and human resource planning being used interchangeably (Thomason 1988) has already been quoted. The quiet subtitling of the Institute of Personnel Management journal *Person-*

nel Management as 'the magazine for human resource professionals' is another example of that process. Is it simply that human resourcing is the old wine of personnel management in new bottles? Karen Legge has suggested that this may be the case (Legge unpublished). For many the suspicion remains that HR is yet another device, the latest fad to provide a moral cloak of respectability concealing the true purpose of business, which is to reduce costs, make a fast buck and get out rich and quick. For others, the overwhelming evidence as shown in this text is of new approaches to managing people at work. Can these features be summarized?

Essentials of human resourcing

The key features and the driving force of HR have been established as:

> Customers
> Quality
> Employees

These are the key words, but to them can be added team-working, mutuality, flexibility, commitment and, of course, trust. In a sense, trust underpins them all, as it does in so much human endeavour that tries to create excellence.

The drive to meet new standards of customer satisfaction and new levels of quality in products or services requires new ways of managing people. At the same time, focusing on customers and quality through employees provides the prospect that the context in which people do their jobs will provide greater levels of purpose and hopefully, therefore, job satisfaction.

There are some key words shown in Figure 15.1 and used in this text which are the fertile ground on which all else might grow. This is the language of human resourcing – and it is now clearly sweeping through even the most die-hard, old-world personnel department.

The personnel function's role

The role of the personnel function in any HR strategy is bound to be

Figure 15.1   The Language of Human Resourcing

crucial. Human resource planning will not take place without the commitment and support of senior executives in the organization.

The essentials described in this book will require day-to-day support to give them coherence in the individual organization. There are a variety of vehicles that can be used. Blakes grid and Coverdale are examples, as are total quality management, bench-marking and quality circles. An alternative would be to learn from other companies and introduce a package tailored to the company's needs.

What you should not do is send everyone on a team-building course. There is no limit to the variety of programmes available – at some cost – from consultants. Managers and employees generally undoubtedly enjoy these experiences but they do not create com-mitment and teams. At most such packages should be seen as a catalyst to change. The secret (if it is a secret!) is in the delivery back at the workplace. Whatever method is adopted, the KISS approach (Keep It Simple, Stupid!) has much to commend it and the principles discussed in this text and set out in Figure 15.2 should provide a guide.

There is much in planning human resources that will cause some pain and heart searching and will not be achieved without risk. Common terms and conditions and extensive team-work training will be expensive and will not be achieved without the support of line managers, including supervisors.

---

1   Committed people are the root of organizational success.

2   All the organization's people at all levels must be treated with respect and dignity if commitment is to be achieved.

3   The values and beliefs of the organization as they are practised (not stated!) form a crucial backdrop to the achievement of commitment and quality.

4   People policies must be integrated into the objectives of the organization to ensure a common purpose.

5   There is within people a huge and largely intapped fund of goodwill and desire for personal fulfilment.

6   Organizations must have a mission, a sense of purpose if people are to give their wholehearted support. No better mission exists than customer service and product quality achieved through team-work.

7   A sound financial base, the aim of all organizations, is achievable through committed people. The aim is however the continuity of the organization above other considerations.

Figure 15.2   Principles of HR

The personnel function has to persuade managers to drop the traditional approaches to people and to work towards a position of mutuality and trust. At the same time questions will have to be asked about why customer satisfaction and quality products or service have not been achieved in the past. This may require the company to think hard about objectives, performance measurement and approaches to reward management. These are likely to be testing tasks.

Finally, it all comes back to belief and therefore culture. Some may find it hard to believe in true team-working, finding satisfaction in the rough and tumble of organizational life. This may apply as much to trade unions, where they are a key part of the organization, as it does to senior managers.

The problem of fads

Of course the HR department, as the driving force behind the development of a human resource strategy, must guard against a dependence on 'fads'. The question to be asked all the time is whether the technique is simply repackaging or whether it provides change of real substance. At the end of the day, management gurus and consultants do not really know what they are doing. Because they are engaged on the novel and innovative, it is inevitable that they will not fully understand the implications of what may be a very good idea. You have to be aware that going down the fads route risks neglecting the underlying culture and beliefs without which change will not be substantial. We also have to be aware that many of Tom Peters' 'excellent' companies would no longer be so regarded. The shine has gone off even Big Blue IBM itself because it forgot its customers, became self-satisfied and found change impossible. It is not easy to keep ahead!

Outsourcing and the human resources department

Many organizations look at the cost of recruitment, training, salary administration, payroll and so on and quickly come to a decision that they can save a lot of money by getting someone outside the organization to contract for the task (Bett 1993). If the whole 'personnel department' is 'outsourced' in this way, the reason may well be the manner in which the personnel department was run. Many old-style personnel departments are unable to throw off their industrial relations 'can't do' culture and find themselves increasingly out of step. If the personnel department can be outsourced, it is because it has relied for its existence on maintaining expensive administrative functions. Many manager colleagues have been irritated by the detached middle-man image. Perhaps the correct response to the outsourcing surge is to go with it, ensuring that contracts are correctly managed and controlled. At the same time, the HR manager will be working on people management strategies that are central to the organization and cannot be outsourced, and in which a significant HR contribution can be made. In addition, the HR manager can contemplate the managerial problems that result from a need to manage a growing number of outsourced activities. This could end up being a new core skill and one which will need developing in managers.

There will be a growing desire in many organizations to outsource an increasing number of traditional personnel management activities. Some learning (particularly of repeatable courses for skills such as word processor training) will be outsourced, as will recruitment, catering, and welfare and counselling services. Outsourcing, though, is unlikely to be a panacea. The HR director should emphasize the difference between strategy and operations. The latter can be outsourced; the former never could. The organization must never relinquish its grip on the activities, systems or information that gave it the edge over its competitor organizations, whether they are strategic or operational. Some areas of welfare activity, such as counselling through an employee assistance programme (EAP), are actually better outsourced than handled internally because the employee recognizes the value of independent advice.

An obvious point can also be stressed – the organization will need well drawn-up contracts and managers appointed to run them. It is rarely possible to outsource and then forget it. Outsourcing has to be looked at carefully and should perhaps be viewed as (to use the jargon!) 'rightsourcing' (Wilcocks 1993).

Empowerment

As we progress to the millennium the talk is all of 'empowerment'. Again, we have to be cautious. W. Edwards Deming, who knows a thing or two about quality organizations, is very sceptical. 'Empowerment? Nonsense! People need to know what their jobs are!' (Deming 1993).

What people seem to mean by empowerment varies dramatically. Is it employee involvement or what happens when middle management jobs are 'de-layered'? Care has to be taken if employees are not to become cynical about empowerment. In an HR environment empowerment is an integral part of a strategy for motivation and commitment. People respond to being asked to undertake tasks which involve assuming greater responsibility. And this, surely, is what empowerment is about – the deliberate and orderly distribution of power and authority to different levels in the organization. It is true that this will mean middle managers' jobs disappearing – but that (despite its benefits) is not the purpose. The HR manager is looking for commitment and enthusiastic support, allied to a concern for product quality and innovation. The cost reductions are an effect, not a reason for making the change. As the HR manager cuts away at managerial levels he will be thinking how he will handle the fallout, such as disenchanted managers and reduced promotion prospects. HR professionals must not resist the inevitable but have to deal with the consequences!

The demographic time bomb

This phrase was commonly used in the 1980s to describe the rapid decline in school leavers that was then in prospect. Well, we got here and perhaps most people will be thankful that there are not a few 100,000 extra unemployed to cause us greater problems.

The real demographic time bomb is the cost of the welfare state caused by an ageing population and the decline in the number of employed creating wealth to pay for it. The number of people over 65 will double in EU countries within 50 years. In 1990, there were 5 working people for every 65-year-old; in 25 years time there will be 4; and in 50 years time 3. It is a remorseless decline with enormous potential for trouble. HR strategies will be required to deal with it.

For example, what about pension schemes that are based on the final year's salary and stop older people moving to less arduous, perhaps shorter-time working.

More part-time work for older people is another necessity but HR strategies which encourage flexibility without resorting to abuse are also required. In the current climate, many organizations solve a problem by retiring older workers. Demographic pressures will soon put a stop to that. How will the HR specialist then deal with the next crisis? The problems of learning and redeployment and of handling the demotion of increasing numbers of employees, who in an earlier age (the 1990s!) would have been 'retired early on health grounds' will all be challenges for the HR department of the future.

Reverse synergy

Everywhere there is a questioning of the gathering together in conglomerates. Organizations are breaking themselves up to enable concentration on key decisions, to speed up change and adaptability and to reduce costs. Perhaps one of the most notable examples of this is the ICI/Zeneca demerger in the UK. The implications of these changes has hardly been realized. Perhaps small is, after all, beautiful and perhaps the 'savings' that come from centralization are illusory when stacked against the cost of inflexibility in decision making. What we are witnessing is the start of an extraordinary process of 'reverse synergy' where the parts, when divided, are greater than the whole!

European Union

Meanwhile waiting in the wings is one organization that does not believe in 'reverse synergy' and certainly wants to empower no one except itself. The effect on HR is going to be substantial – whatever happens to the European Worker Councils, TEMPUS (restructuring of education) and Petra (network of youth training), the Mastricht Social Protocol and the rest. Organizations will have to be concerned about their effect on costs and competitiveness in the European economies. The bureaucracy and influence of Europe is hardly likely to continue to allow UK opt-outs (which are anyway undesirable). There is trouble brewing here and HR directors, like everyone else, will have to meet the directive requirements efficiently and positively and face the challenge of Europe head-on.

HR-speak

One area that should concern the HR professional is the tendency for jargon to spring up around any new subject. So we have downsizing, performance drivers, clean-sheet solutions, empowerment, competences, re-engineering, de-layering, sharing, missions and mission statements, and outsourcing, among many others. This 'corporate graffiti', as Tom Roberts of London Business School has dubbed it (thereby making his own contribution), should concern the human resources manager. While new ideas often need to be expressed in a new language, 'downsizing' is usually a sanitized substitute for 'redundancy', just as 'marketplace' is a way of saying 'market'. People used to work in an 'office', which became a 'work station' and is now an 'enterprise environment'. We have to take care that in using this sort of jargon we do not miss an essential message of HR, which is openness and honesty. If we say that we have 'a shared corporate philosophy leading to empowerment through re-engineering and rightsizing' when we mean 'we are giving more work to some people and sacking middle managers' – then we should perhaps take stock. It is all too easy to use the jargon to give the impression of being up to date and having something snappy to say, when the reality may be something quite different. HR managers should beware of fashionable HR speak – it will quickly lead to discredit.

And to end . . .

This book has stressed the human aspects of managing organizations. Machiavelli, a much-maligned thinker, knew the realities and tried to formulate a process to come to terms with them. He said:

> The problem with any change is that you are assured of the criticism of those who prosper under the old and fear the loss of prosperity under the new, while not being able to achieve the support of those who may prosper under the new.

To many, HR will seem a mirror of the rise of the 'new right'. Of course it is not so new and many Japanese and US companies and perhaps Michelin in France will believe that they were there before the rest of us. If this is the case it is hardly surprising. There are many who will not mourn the passing of the 'old left'. Perhaps there will always be contradictions within work between the various stakeholders, but who would wish to argue the case for 1950s and 1960s collectivism as a method of achieving economic success and personal fulfilment?

It is up to HR proponents to argue the case. Personnel management is done *to* employees while human resourcing is done *by* employees.

Amid this uncertainty and Legge and Gowler's respectable scepticism, there is, for me, more than a glimmer of hope. Quality and service – perhaps in these two aspects lies the secret. Employees have to be part of an economically successful venture and people's continuity is not helped if that success is threatened. But perhaps quality and service can give to all jobs that ingredient of humane purpose that will encourage self-respect and integrity in a company's dealings.

So the conflicts will exist and there will be occasions when tough decisions have to be taken – continuity requires that. But this 'tough love' or 'care which does not shy away from tough decisions' (Legge unpublished) need not frighten the HR enthusiast. What idyllic past has been preferable in terms of both economic success and human fulfilment to the hope held out by HR to both human and economic peformance within the company?

Can we do it? At a US conference in California I heard one speaker say 'We in the East are going to win and you are going to lose in the West. There is nothing you can do about it because to us human resourcing is not something that is *done* to people it is a *belief* and you do not and cannot understand that.' With that chilling thought we have to pick up the challenge. The personnel function is the organizational force that has to drive and plan a human resource strategy to the point where the prosperity and benefit is there for all (customers, employees and other stakeholders) to see.

References and Further Reading

ANDERSON G. and others. 'Appraisal without form filling'. *Personnel Management*. February 1987.

ARDREY R. *The territorial imperative*. London, Collins, 1967.

ARGYRIS G. *Integrating the individual and the organization*. Wiley, 1964.

ARKIN A. 'The workforce who got sick of absenteeism'. *PM Plus*. Vol 4, No 11, November 1993

ARMSTRONG G. 'Priorities for a trade union review'. *Personnel Management*. December 1987.

ARMSTRONG M. *Handbook of human resource management*. London, Kogan Page, 1987.

ARMSTRONG M. and MURLIS H. *Reward Management*. London, Institute of Personnel Management/Kogan Page, 1988.

ATKINSON J. 'Flexibility – planning for an uncertain future'. *Manpower Policy and Practice*. Spring 1985.

ATKINSON J. 'Flexibility, uncertainty and manpower management'. *IMS Report* 89, 1985.

BASSETT P. 'A moral edge forward – interview with J. Edmonds of GMB'. *Financial Times*. August 1987.

BATSTONE and others. 'Unions on the board'. *Employee Relations*. Vol 5, No 5, 1983.

BAYLEY J. 'Customer service – a philosophy not a department'. *Personnel Management*. March 1987.

BEAUMONT P. *The decline of trade union organization*. London, Croom Helm, 1987.

BELBIN R. M. *Management teams: why they succeed or fail*. London, Heinemann, 1981.

BENNIS W. G. 'Leadership theory – the problem of authority'. *Administrative Science Quarterly*. December 1959.

BENNISON M. and CASSON J. *Manpower Planning Handbook*. Brighton, IMS, 1984.

BETT M. 'Pioneering a new role for Personnel'. *Personnel Management*. November 1993.

BLAKE R. R. and MOUTON J. S. *The managerial grid*. Houston, Gulf, 1964.

BOWEY A. *Handbook of salary and wage systems*. Aldershot, Gower, 1983.

BRAMHAM J. *Practical Manpower Planning*. London, Institute of Personnel Management, 1975, 4th ed., 1988.

BUCHANAN D. A. and HUCZYNSKI A. A. *Organizational Behaviour*. Hemel Hempstead, Prentice Hall/IPM, 1985.

BURGOYNE J. 'Management development for individuals and organizations'. *Personnel Management*. June 1988.

CARR J. *New roads to equality: contract compliance for the UK*. London, Fabian Society, 1987

CARTWRIGHT D. and ZANDER A. *Group Dynamics*. London, Tavistock, 1968.

CHILD J. *Organisation: a guide to problems and practice*. London, Harper and Row, 1984.

COLES R. 'Merit Pay at Ferranti'. IPM Conference Paper, 1985.

COLLARD R. and DALE B. 'Quality circles – why they break down and why they hold up'. *Personnel Management*. February 1985.

CONFEDERATION OF BRITISH INDUSTRY. *A strategy for the development of an industry-education partnership*. London, CBI, 1988.

CONFERENCE BOARD. *Does Quality Work?*. Review of studies into Total Quality. New York, Conference Board, 1994.

CROSS M. *Towards the flexible craftsman*. London, Technical Change Centre, 1985.

CYERT R. M. and MARCH J. C. *A behavioural theory of the firm*. Hemel Hempstead, Prentice Hall, 1963.

DAY M. 'Managerial competence and the Charter initiative'. *Personnel Management*. August 1988.

DEMING W. EDWARDS. *Out of the Crisis*. Cambridge, Cambridge University Press, 1988.

DEVELOPMENT COUNCIL OF SWEDEN. *Volvo-Kalmar revisited*. Development Council of Sweden, 1984.

DRENNAN D. 'How to make the bad news less bad and the good

news great'. *Personnel Management*. August 1988 (see also the piece by Len Peach in the same issue).

DRUCKER P. F. *The practice of management*. London, Heinemann, 1955.

EASTERBY-SMITH M. *Evaluation of management education, training and development*. Aldershot, Gower/IPM, 1986.

ELTIS W. 'How Marx maimed Britain'. Unionism section of *Managment Today*, London, August 1983.

EQUAL OPPORTUNITIES COMMISSION. *A model equal opportunities policy*. London, EOC, 1985.

EQUAL OPPORTUNITIES REVIEW. Nos. 5–10. London, EOC, 1986.

ERBAN P. 'How they manage performance in Windsor'. *Personnel Management*. February 1989.

FIEDLER F. E. *A theory of leadership effectiveness*. Maidenhead, McGraw Hill, 1974.

FISHER R. and URY W. *Getting to yes*. London, Hutchinson, 1983.

FITZ-ENZ J. *Human Value Management*. California, Jossey-Bass Inc, 1990.

FITZ-ENZ J. *Benchmarking Performance*. California, Jossey-Bass Inc, 1993.

FOWLER A. 'When Chief Executives Discover HRM'. *Personnel Management*. January 1987.

FOX A. *Beyond contract: work, power and trust relations*. London, Faber, 1974.

FOX A. *Time span of discretion theory: an appraisal*. London, Penguin, 1972.

GALBRAITH J. K. *The anatomy of power*. London, Hamish Hamilton, 1984.

GAPPER J. S. 'Staff complain over customer care schemes'. *Financial Times*. 4 May 1989.

GILL D. and UNGERSON B. *Challenge of equal value*. London, Insitute of Personnel Management, 1984.

GOFFEE R. and SCASE R. *Reluctant managers*. London, Unwin Hyman, 1989.

GOLDSMITH W. and CLUTTERBUCK D. *The Winning Streak*.

London, Penguin, 1985.

GOLZEN G. 'Reward the stars – but what of the rest?' *The Times.* November 1988.

GOW I. 'Raiders, invaders or just good traders'. *Accounting.* March 1986.

GOWLER D. 'Values, contracts and job satisfaction'. *Personnel Review.* Autumn 1974.

GOWLER D. and LEGGE K. 'Images of employees in company reports – do company chairmen view their most valuable asset as valuable?'. *Personnel Review.* Vol 15, No 5, 1986.

GRANADA GUILDHALL LECTURES 'The role of trade unions – a critique'. London, Granada, 1980.

GUEST D. and KENNY T. *Techniques and strategies in personnel management.* London, Institute of Personnel Management, 1983.

GWENT TEC. See *Standards for IiP Consultants.*

HANDY C. B. *The age of unreason.* London, Hutchinson, 1989.

HANDY C. B. *Understanding organizations.* Penguin, 1981 and 1985.

HARPER S. (Ed). *Personnel Management Handbook.* Aldershot, Gower, 1987.

HARRIS H. *The right to manage – industrial relations policies of American business.* University of Wisconsin, 1982

HARVEY-JONES J. *Making it happen – reflections on leadership.* London, Collins, 1988.

HASTINGS C. and others. *The superteam solution.* Aldershot, Gower, 1986.

HENDRY C. 'Banking on HRM to respond to change'. *Personnel Management.* November 1987.

HERZBERG F. *Work and the nature of man.* New York, Staples Press, 1966.

HODGSON A. 'Deming's never-ending road to quality'. *Personnel Management,* July 1987.

HOGG C. 'Customer care programmes'. *Personnel Management.* Factsheet 13, January 1989.

HOGG C. 'Peformance appraisal'. *Personnel Management.* Factsheet 3, March 1988.

HOGG C. 'Stress management' *Personnel Management.* Factsheet 7, July 1988.

INCOME DATA SERVICES. 'Supervisors of manual workers'. IDS Study 346, 1985.

INDUSTRIAL PARTICIPATION ASSOCIATION. '1992 – Employee Involvement and Participation: Which way will it go?' *EEC Newsletter*, August 1988.

INDUSTRIAL SOCIETY. *Flexibility – how British industry is changing to survive.* London, Industrial Society, 1986.

INSTITUTE OF PERSONNEL MANAGEMENT DIGEST 'Aspects of Motivation – or treating people as you'd treat yourself'. IPM *Digest* No. 269, December 1987.

INSTITUTE OF PERSONNEL MANAGEMENT *Performance appraisal revisited* London, IPM, 1986.

INSTITUTE OF PERSONNEL MANAGEMENT *Practical Participation and Involvement*, Vols. 1 to 5. London, IPM, 1981–2.

INSTITUTE OF PERSONNEL MANAGEMENT 'Who'd be an equal opportunities manager?'. *Personnel Management.* April 1988.

JACQUES E. *General theory of bureaucracy.* London, Heinemann, 1976.

JAY A. *Management and Machiavelli.* London, Hutchinson, 1987.

KERRY I. P. J. and REID M. A. *Training interventions.* London, Institute of Personnel Management, 1986.

KOCHAN A. and others. *The transformation of American industrial relations.* New York, Basic Books, 1986.

KOTTER J. P. *Power in management.* New York, Amacom, 1979.

LAWRENCE P. R. and LORSCH J. W. *Organization and environment.* Harvard Business School, 1967.

LEEK R. 'Flexible manning in practice' *Manpower Policy and Practice.* Summer 1985.

LEGGE K. *Power, innovation and problem solving in personnel management.* Maidenhead, McGraw Hill, 1978.

LEGGE K. 'Human resource management – a critical analysis', (unpublished).

LICKERT R. *New patterns of management.* Maidenhead, McGraw Hill, 1961.

LUKES S. *Power – a radical view'* London, Macmillan, 1981. (Studies in sociology).

LUPTON T. (ed) *Payment Systems*. London, Penguin, 1972.

MACHIAVELLI N. *The Prince*. London, Penguin, 1967. (Translated).

MANN S. 'Why open learning can be a turn off'. *Personnel Management*. January 1988.

MARCHINGTON M. '4 faces of employee consultation'. *Personnel Management*. May 1988.

MARGERISON C. 'Delivering success in management development'. *Journal of Management Development*. Vol 1, No 3, 1982.

MARTIN P. and NICHOLLS J. *Creating a committed workforce*. London, Institute of Personnel Management, 1988.

MASLOW A. H. 'A theory of human motivation'. *US Psychological Review*. Vol 50, No 4, 1943.

MATTESON M. T. and IVANCEVICK J. M. *Management classics*. Goodyear, 1981.

MAYO E. *Report on studies at Hawthorne works of the Western Electric Co Chicago 1927–1932*. Harvard Business School, 1933.

McGREGOR D. *The human side of enterprise*. Maidenhead, McGraw Hill, 1960

METCALF D. 'Can unions survive in the private sector?' Working Paper No. 1120. London, LSE, 1989.

MILLER P. 'Strategic HRM'. *Personnel Management*. February 1989.

MINTZBERG H. *Power in and around organizations*. Hemel Hempstead, Prentice Hall, 1983.

MINTZBERG H. *Structure of organizations*. Hemel Hempstead, Prentice Hall, 1979.

MUMFORD A. (Ed). *Handbook of Management Development*. Aldershot, Gower, 1986.

MURLIS H. and GRIST J. *Towards Single Status*. London, British Institute of Management (B1), 1976.

NATIONAL ECONOMIC DEVELOPMENT OFFICE. *Competence and competition*. London, NEDO, 1984.

NICHOLLS T. and ARMSTRONG P. *Workers divided*. London, Fontana, 1976.

PASCALE, R. T. and ATHOS A. G. *The art of Japanese management*. London, Penguin, 1982.

PATRICK J. 'What's new in training'. *Personnel Management.* September 1984.

PETER L. J. and HULL R. *The Peter principle.* London, Pan, 1970.

PETERS T. J. and AUSTIN N. K. *A passion for excellence.* London, Collins, 1985.

PETERS T. J. *Thriving on chaos.* London, Macmillan, 1988.

PETERS T. J. and WATERMAN R. H. (Jnr). *In search of excellence – lessons from America's best-run companies.* New York, Harper and Row, 1982.

PETTIGREW A. *Is corporate culture manageable?* Centre for Corporate Strategy and Change, University of Warwick, 1986.

PETTIGREW A. *The politics of organisational decision making.* London, Tavistock, 1973.

PEUGEOT. Details of the settlement on attendance pay quoted in *The Times.* 28 February 1989.

PFEFFER J. *Power in organisations.* London, Pitman, 1981.

'Plan for modern apprentices'. *PM Plus.* Vol 14, No 12, December 1993.

PLASTOW D. 'Brief and to the point – comment on employee communications'. *Personnel Management.* September 1988.

PM PLUS. See 'Plan for modern apprentices'.

POLLERT A. *Flexible firm – a policy in search of practice.* IRRU, University of Warwick, 1988.

PRIESTLEY J. B. *The English.* London, Heinemann, 1973.

PRYOR R. and MAYO A. 'A fresh approach to performance appraisal'. *Personnel Management.* June 1985.

PURCELL J. 'Is anybody listening to the corporate personnel department?' *'Personnel Management.* September 1985.

REDDIN W. J. *The best of Bill Reddin.* London, Institute of Personnel Management, 1982.

ROBERTS C. *Harmonisation – whys and wherefores.* London, Institute of Personnel Management, 1985.

ROBERTSON I. T. and SMITH M. *Motivation and job design.* London, Institute of Personnel Management, 1985.

RODGER D. and MABEY C. 'BT's leap forward from assessment centres'. *Personnel Management.* July 1987.

ROWBOTTOM R. and BILLIS D. 'Cutting out management overlap'. *Personnel Management.* November 1987.

SANDWICH P. 'Absenteeism'. *Drake Review.* Vol 3, No 1, 1987.

SAUNDERS G. *The committed organisation.* Aldershot, Gower, 1984.

SCHEANE D. 'Beyond Bureaucracy'. *Management Research.*

SCHEIN E. H. *Organizational psychology.* Hemel Hempstead, Prentice Hall, 1970.

SCHUMACHER E. F. *Small is Beautiful.* London, Blond and Briggs, 1973.

SKAE J. 'Cash rewards not perks'. *The Times.* 23 June 1988.

SLOMAN M. 'On the job training – a costly poor relation'. *Personnel Management.* February 1989.

SMITH D. 'Unions left out of the market'. *Sunday Times.* 26 March 1989.

SMITH I. *The management of remuneration – paying for effectiveness.* London, IPM/Gower, 1983.

SPARROW P. and PETTIGREW A. 'How Halfords put its HRM into top gear'. *Personnel Management.* June 1988.

Standards for IiP Consultants. Gwent TEC, 1993.

STEWART R. *Contrasts in management.* Maidenhead, McGraw Hill, 1976.

STOREY J. (ed). *New perspectives in human resource management.* London, Routledge, forthcoming.

TAYLOR F. W. *Principles of scientific management.* New York, Harper, 1911.

TAYLOR P. 'Sickness absence: facts and misconceptions'. *Journal of the Royal College of Physicians.* July 1974.

'Team briefing: Practical steps in employee communication'. *Industrial Relations Review and Report.* February 1986.

THOMAS M. 'Coming to terms with the customer'. *Personnel Management.* February 1987.

THOMASON G. *A textbook of human resource management.* London, Institute of Personnel Management, 1988.

THOMSON F. '7 deadly sins of briefing groups'. *Personnel Management.* February 1983.

THRASHER F. *The Gang.* Chicago, Chicago University Press, 1927.

TOFFLER A. *Future shock.* London, Bodley Head, 1970.

TOFFLER A. *The third wave.* London, Pan, 1980.

TORRINGTON D. and HALL L. *Personnel Management – a new approach.* Hemel Hempstead, Prentice Hall/IPM, 1987.

TOWERS B. and others. 'Do worker directors work?' *Employment Gazette*. September 1981.

TRADE UNION RESEARCH UNIT. *The flexible firm and the shape of jobs to come*. Oxford, Ruskin College, 1984.

TRAINING COMMISSION. *The funding of vocational education and training: some early research findings*. Background note no. 2, a survey conducted for the TC by Deloitte Haskins and Sells together with IFF. 1988.

VROOM V. H. *Work and motivation*. New York, Wiley, 1964.

VROOM V. H. and DECI E. L. *Management and motivation*. London, Penguin, 1970 (includes excellent reviews of other studies, eg Blake and Mouton).

WALLUM P. 'Financial incentives for top executives'. *Personnel Management*. April 1983.

WALTON R. E. 'From control to commitment in the workplace'. *Harvard Business Review*. March 1985.

WEBER M. *The theory of social and economic organisation*. London, Oxford University Press, 1947.

WHITE R. and LIPPITT R. *Autocracy and democracy*. New York, Harper & Row, 1960.

WHYTE W. H. *The organisation man*. London, Penguin, 1955.

WHYTE W. H. 'What's new in pay? *Personnel Magazine*. February 1985.

WICKENS P. *The Road to Nissan*. London, Macmillan, 1988.

WILCOCKS L. *Research News – Templeton College Oxford*. Michaelmas 1993.

WINTOUR P. 'Employer's right to communicate'. *Industrial Society*. September 1988.

WRONG D. *Power – its forms, bases and uses*. Oxford, Blackwell, 1979.

Index